I
AM
NOT
FINISHED
YET

DORSHA GREY

authorHOUSE®

AuthorHouse™
1663 Liberty Drive
Bloomington, IN 47403
www.authorhouse.com
Phone: 1-800-839-8640

Published by AuthorHouse 10/17/2014

ISBN: 978-1-4969-4649-2 (sc)
ISBN: 978-1-4969-4650-8 (e)

THIS BOOK IS DEDICATED TO MY SON,
CHRISTOPHER, AND HIS WIFE MELISSA.
YOU ARE THE LOVES OF MY LIFE.

CONTENTS

Special acknowledgements ix

Special thank you to: xi

Introduction xiii

One: Make It Count 1

Two: Negatives And Positives 21

Three: Don't Get Caught Up...32

Four: If I Can Think It – I Can Do It. Be Driven!.....................47

Five: Know Your Worth 57

Six: A Swift Kick In The Butt 71

Seven: Sum It Up 85

Eight: Be The Best You...105

About The Author..111

SPECIAL ACKNOWLEDGEMENTS

TO ALL OF MY FAMILY: THANK YOU FOR BEING IN MY LIFE AND FOR BEING WHO YOU ARE. I LOVE YOU ALL.

A SPECIAL THANK YOU TO MY MOTHER. WITHOUT YOU, THIS BOOK WOULD NOT BE POSSIBLE.

FRIENDS WHO ARE SPECIAL TO ME: NOEL COLLINS AND FAMILY, CIDNEY WALKER AND FAMILY, DESEAN LEE, RACHAL LEE, HELEN AND WILLIAM BREWER AND FAMILY, THE BURNS FAMILY, ERROL WILKERSON, RHONDA THOMAS WOOTEN, PEGGY HILL AND FAMILY, AND RICKY METOYER AND FAMILY. THANK YOU FOR ALWAYS BEING THERE, AND MOST OF ALL, THANK YOU FOR YOUR PRAYERS.

SPECIAL THANK YOU TO:

DR. COSENZA (ONE OF THE WORLD'S BEST SURGEONS). YOU SAVED MY LIFE. I WILL FOREVER BE GRATEFUL.

GEORGE N. FALLIERAS, MD. ONE OF THE FINEST DOCTORS IN THE MEDICAL PROFESSION. YOU HAVE GREAT UNDERSTANDING OF YOUR FIELD, AND YOU TREAT YOUR PATIENTS WITH THE BEST CARE.

DR. ELLSWORTH GRANT. YOU ARE AN AMAZING LISTENER. YOU ARE A MAN OF PATIENCE. YOU ARE A MAN OF GREAT KNOWLEDGE. YOU ARE TRULY A PROFESSIONAL.

INTRODUCTION

As I sit here today, June 4, 2014, on this lumpy futon which serves as my sofa and my bed, I can't help but reflect on life and what it takes to live. I think about the <u>past</u>, <u>present</u>, and <u>future</u>. My reflection is only on the good. What *has changed* what matters, what *can change* what matters, and what *will change* what matters.

We think we know ourselves, but there are people we connect with that know what we're capable of and may realize our potential before we see it. You have some that will point it out to you and help you get there. Then, you have others that will look at you, smile, *think about it* – then casually walk away, and maybe even hope you don't figure it out.

We may even know our creative mind, gift, or talent, but don't know how to achieve our goals or even where to start.

Then we have the procrastinator. The one who knows what to do but continues to find the reasons – I mean excuses (sorry) – to not start NOW.

I was the procrastinator. But something very serious happened to me on March 16, 2014 that cannot be forgotten and will forever change my life to where I choose not to procrastinate with anything of importance ever again. I will no longer bind and shackle myself – creating my own limitations. I will be unlimited with ability. I will no longer set boundaries for myself. I am going to fill the "blank pages."

On March 16, 2014, I experienced the worse pain I could imagine in my abdominal area. I called my neighbor and asked her to come over. She saw me crying and balled up in (what I call) a knot. She immediately called paramedics and I was transported by the Los Angeles Fire Department to Good Samaritan Hospital in Los Angeles. I was diagnosed in emergency with a bleeding ulcer and then told, because of this ulcer, had another week passed, I would have died. I was scheduled for emergency surgery for the next morning. After surgery, I was told I had a tumor in my stomach that was cancerous - stage three. I had a total gastrectomy. No, I did not know I was that sick. About three weeks before going to the Good Samaritan, I felt sick and took myself to emergency (a different hospital) because my stomach was bothering me and I was throwing up. I sat there for seven hours (I had no health insurance) and had not been seen by a doctor. I felt so bad I didn't want to wait any longer, so I went home. Prior to this, I thought I was just going through stressful times because of my money situation, and I had also recently lost a six year old niece to a fatal automobile accident. I wasn't visibly bleeding from anywhere so I was not aware of the ulcer. With no health insurance, I hadn't seen a doctor in a while –and I never had a physical examination. I am not thrilled with going to county facilities, but I will tell you this, if you feel bad enough, please go somewhere for treatment and stay until you are seen by a physician. Even better – make sure you have some kind of health insurance in place. Do not self-diagnose thinking you have one thing, because, obviously, it can be something a lot more severe or life-threatening.

With that said, this is why this book is in your hands today. This work, this piece right here, should have been done some time ago. I have had the makings of this book in my head (my brain) since the summer of 2013. But three days after my surgery, I came to one conclusion, that I would not leave this world (whenever that time may be) without sharing and expressing – *on a wide scale* (through publication) how I feel and care about people and want to know they are okay. In August of 2013, I wrote "The Final Test (No One Is Exempt)," and, "The Final Test Is a Reality." I personally gave these writings to about ten people I know.

People often ask me if I've written anything else. Well, *here I am*. I have something to say, and **I plan to make it count**.

In this writing I will tell you how I got to where I am today, and I am going to let you know how I will arrive at my tomorrow and fulfill goals for my future.

In this writing you will have a better idea of what not to do, as well as understand how to fill your "blank pages," if you have any.

I am going to put it straight. I am going to lay it down.

But I'll let you know this up front, if you are looking for perfection in a book or a person, you may as well put this book down right now because I am not perfect, nor do I plan to be. I do, however, know what counts, and I am going to make it happen. So if you're down, and want to make it happen too – we can do this together.

Check it out!

ONE

MAKE IT COUNT

I will start by saying I am a business-minded person. I am presently a licensed real estate salesperson living in Los Angeles, California. I have been licensed as a sales agent since 1996, with a previous background in banking. Sounds alright, huh? So how did I end up with a lot less money than I would like to have, and living in a 700 square foot apartment? Seriously! I presently do not have the balances (available cash) I would like to have in my bank accounts. But this is going to change considerably before the completion of this book. I am going to prove to you what drive, positive intention with a purpose, motivation, and focus will do for the goals you set for yourself.

If you are where I am today we are going to stay on course of our plans and successfully reach our intended goals for a more rewarding and satisfying life. We will take advantage of opportunities right then and there (seizing moments), no procrastinating, and will actively seek and find resources needed to put our plans into action. We will be a part of a support group, or hire a personal coach or consultant to keep us motivated. We will take a vow to not sit around and sulk for any length of time when things are not going as well as planned. Because when stuff happens (and it will) we will *be strong enough to find the solution*.

A little background information on who Dorsha Grey is.

I came from humble beginnings, a large family. I have three sisters and three brothers. My parents were not very well off financially, but we never missed a meal, our clothes were always clean, and my mother kept the house spotless. I stayed in school and was a good student. I made Who's Who of American High School students several times, and was an Honor Student. I even received a letter from Mensa in the 12th grade. I have been working on a regular basis since I was sixteen years old, and began working in the banking industry at the age of eighteen. I have been employed at least 97% of my adult life, and I am a knowledgeable and intelligent person. I have one adult son, Christopher, who married a beautiful woman by the name of Melissa Elena on June 7, 2014. I feel grateful to have such a wonderful son that was raised well and made the right decisions in life, and I appreciate all of my family very much.

But at this moment, I have some personal adjustments to make, as you know, because I didn't take advantage of certain opportunities given to me the moment of presentation. I did not seek further resources needed to put certain plans into action, and put into play procrastination/poor time management/not controlling my activities to get maximum results/lack of discipline/mentally dwelling on matters not relevant or pertinent to my business and goals (which all caused a *severe* financial slump). I could add a few more slashes (///), but I think you get my point. If this is you right now, you feel me. This situation can be changed though, and it can be right and tight **within 90 days.**

It can take a short period of time to remedy situations and certain circumstances in our life. The main problem is how long we take before anything is done to correct what could be wrong, and what/who we allow to get in our way. *Whether we want to realize it or not, we are the solution to much of what is not right about what*

2

we don't appreciate with what is going on in our life. **IT'S ABOUT CHOICES.**

One thing I do to keep myself on course daily is listen to Bishop Charles E. Blake, pastor of West Angeles Church of God in Christ, every morning and every night. I have Bishop Blake's CD of the 11:00am service of February 2, 2014, and believe me - it is POWERFUL!!! I do mental visualization for 30 minutes in the morning, and 30 minutes of positive and powerful visualization before I go to sleep. I also listen to a Success Magazine CD <u>every single day</u>.

Success Magazine, and Darren Hardy's CD's are very helpful, and I feel they are necessary to read and listen to – *especially for the entrepreneur.* I assure that you would not be disappointed. The Success Magazine CD is my main driving force right now. The Success series is my personal trainer presently because it is within my budget, and I have a variety of the best trainers and coaches in this program. I get a wealth of information from the best, and it makes me feel as if I am already a part of a group that has achieved what I am aspiring to accomplish to get *back on target* in having satisfaction, fulfillment and success in *my life.* You want to be among the best on your path to success. The subscription is well worth it. Even when I am able to afford a personal one-on-one coach again, I will continue to keep my Success Magazine subscription in place.

I was not paid to say this. I just believe in sharing information that can help others, and sharing information that gets to the point. I will give many other tips in this book that you may be able to benefit from.

In this book you will have assignments and research on subjects I will give you. It is important to do these exercises. The assignments have very valuable information that is relevant to what you are reading in this book.

I intended this to be a one book message, but as I look at all I have to impart, another writing will follow. You will need answers to your questions, and you will sometimes have questions for your answers.

LIFE IS ALRIGHT, BUT…..

Things may become uncertain, probable, unstable, and not steady. You may sense unlikelihood in some situations. You may become fearful, worry may set in. Fright, disbelief… problems may occur. You don't have immediate answers. Your tone and mood changes, your positive thinking changes, stress and depression may arise. Your personal world has been temporarily restructured. Where is this strong, confident person that used to be me? How do I find that person again? Where do I start? How do I begin? Is there anyone that understands?

Psalm 27, 1-3

"The Lord is my light and my salvation; whom shall I fear? The Lord is the strength of my life; of whom shall I be afraid?

When the wicked came against me to eat up my flesh, my enemies and foes, they stumbled and fell.

Though an army may encamp against me my heart shall not fear; though war may rise against me, in this I will be confident."

You will fear no one. You will be afraid of no one. You have strength. You have confidence.

You were not born with fear. You were born **to be** strong and confident. *Psalm 29:11 says, "The Lord will give strength to His people; the Lord will bless His people with peace."*

This is how we are going to start. Say this right now: "**I am going to have an absolutely amazing day!**" Say it. Mean it. Believe it. Own it!

You will not bind yourself anymore. You will not shackle yourself anymore. You will not cause your own limitations. You are boundless, limitless… vast.

Anything is possible because *you* create it. When we let doors get shut in our face…we created that. No more doors will be shut in our face! We will be prepared for any situation, any advantage, any benefit, and any opportunity we set forth to have. We will be prepared with **strength**, **confidence**, and **knowledge**.

As an adult, we have to be our own person. We have to think for ourselves, do for ourselves, and be personally accountable. Your brain is in **your** head. You control it. No one else. Most of all: you need your brain to think, to be, and to have. Don't ever let anyone take that away from you. If you choose to leave with only one thing from this writing – choose this.

We all know knowledge is key (know/knowledge). You feel me family? Know/knowledge. Webster's New World Dictionary has said this about the word knowledge: 1) the fact or state of knowing; 2) range of information or understanding; 3) what is known; learning, and 4) the body of facts, etc. accumulated by humanity – **to (the best of) one's knowledge** as far as one knows. This is knowledge defined.

We perish from the lack of……… Exactly. Knowledge. So why do we suffer? We **know** what we have to do. We **know** full well we are not going to get that job, that client, that sale if we are not prepared. We **know** we are not going to score well on the SAT exam if we are not prepared. We **know** we are not going to successfully complete our college studies on time and graduate with our class if we are not prepared with the knowledge needed to do so. You may not have the relationship you want with someone in particular if you do not have a certain amount of knowledge to go forth and deeper with that individual. Am I right? **We have to own it!**

Your mind is a gold mine. Your mind is priceless. No matter who you are. ***You are so valuable***. Everyone has this ability. And maybe, just maybe, it may take some a little longer than others, but believe me when I tell you this….we all have this ability. There is <u>intelligence</u>, and <u>knowledge</u>, and good <u>in everyone</u>. Especially you. You <u>are</u> priceless. You are precious. You are beautiful, and you are loved. You may not have someone telling you this every day, but guess what? You *are* beautiful. Forget the physical. That is not what I am saying here. I am talking about you <u>as a person</u>. **What's inside… this is my subject.**

By the way….what is inside? In you, I could probably see space (the freedom to be). Someone that could be bursting with happiness at any given moment if they wanted to. Someone who could love to love. I see a mind with many thoughts. I see a heart that could be a treasure already….or, if allowed. I see someone who would love to give, and maybe even take some good things that are given to you. I see someone who would love to share. I see someone who wants to breathe - freshness and new. I see someone who wants to see many others like them…..like… what you have to offer right now, and for that someone to be okay with that. I see you. You are like me. We are human. We breathe, we live, and we love. We want to be loved – the right way. We want to understand. We want to be understood. We want to be.

Here is something you may not know. No one is perfect. And if you think you are---that's a flaw right there. Not even the so-called perfectionist is perfect. That's right, I said it. I'm bad like that. I speak my mind.

So what's up with you? Where are you going? Do you know? If you do, please take a sheet of paper and write down the ten (10) most important things you would like to accomplish within three months, six months, nine months, and one year. If you do not know where you are going, think about it – seriously. Then get a sheet a paper and write those thoughts down in the order of importance of desired completion for a 12 month calendar year. Put your paper aside. We will come back to this later.

You have to drive yourself. No one can physically get inside of your body to move and propel you to do what you need to do to stay motivated to succeed at what you want to have and be in life. (I am serious. Stop playing. Get your mind out of the gutter if that is where it is right now. I am not talking about your morning" quicky" in bed. Really!)

Anyway, we need to know [upfront] what is required in our chosen field. Whether it is an occupation, a particular degree in studies you would like to master, or owning a business – you need to know this completely before pursuing the endeavor. It doesn't matter what age you are - you do not have time to waste, so know going in what is needed to be successful in the venture you set out to accomplish. If you do not know already – then this is an assignment for you. These facts are crucial – extremely important, and cannot be denied. You must have this knowledge in hand. There is no point in reading this book or any other book along these lines if you do not feel this is necessary.

Example: Several years ago, after leaving real estate full-time, I began working as a leasing consultant leasing high-end/luxury apartments with a property management employment agency. I had a very good sales background (I had years of real estate sales experience), so I thought, surely if I could sell property – I could lease. I was an excellent leasing consultant. And I was excellent because I figured this one thing: this would be easy because I don't have to go and get the business – the business would come to me. And it did. I knew how to place very effective advertisement on the internet. I had the personality, the professionalism - the charm. Once I have enough background information and know what people want – the rest is usually easy. I may have to "tip the scale" so to speak sometimes to get them to make a decision – but I was already good at that. I was courteous, friendly, and knew my position well. Leasing rentals is a "piece of cake" compared to hardcore real estate sales, and if the availability is there – for me to lease three units a week, was a cool walk in the park. I was smart, sharp, well dressed, and polished. One day, I decided to apply for a permanent position in property management with a company in Hollywood, but one thing stopped me. That piece of paper. A bachelor's degree from a college or university. Had I passed by doors that required this piece of paper before and got in? Of course I had. Did this position state a four year degree was needed? Sure it did. I interviewed with two people. The first gentleman was impressed with my résumé, and he admired me as a person. He wanted to see me in the position. He told me one thing before leaving the room. He said, "I think you are the best person for the job, but the decision maker in this hiring process is big on degrees, and if anything stops him from hiring you, it would probably be this reason alone." I interviewed with this gentleman next. He was impressed with my background and résumé as well, and said I had a strong presentation, but he wanted a person with a four year college degree in the position.

You see, no matter the background or experience, I did not exactly have what was required to get hired with this particular company. Many companies hire for future openings from *existing* personnel, and feel degrees are necessary for advanced occupations when it comes to certain strengths and knowledge in a field. There is nothing wrong with this. Employee retention is good for business, and, of course, having someone on board who would like to grow with the company and has the ability to do so is a plus from the beginning of the professional relationship. One cannot dispute that decision.

Did I have the knowledge in place to land this job? Yes, I had knowledge of the position I applied for, but I did not have the required degree. I had not completed my college studies at that time. And I missed a great opportunity. Everyone I met that morning, from the receptionist on, would have been people I know I would have enjoyed working with, and the environment was very professional. I had no excuse for not being prepared. I had decades to accomplish completing that degree, but didn't. Know what you need upfront to go as far as you want to go. You never know when you would have to go corporate, and you never know how long you are going to stay corporate. Look at the bright side. Learning is fun. Education is key.

Why didn't I get my degree sooner? I felt I needed to work. I needed to have money coming in at a young age. There was lack of money in my household and I wanted to help my family. I didn't want us to be in need any longer. I was the first of my mother's children to own an automobile. I was 18 years old. My first full-time job was with Bank of America. My office was located at 525 S. Flower Street in Los Angeles. You see, there was no car in our family. We were all on the bus. In the heat, in the rain, and the cold. To go to the grocery store we walked several blocks. To go to the mall…we took the bus. To go to school – the bus. Going to church – we walked about half a mile. So my thinking at the time was to contribute to the household. As I look back, I can say, if I had to do it over again, I would have stayed on the bus, enrolled in a university, worked a part-time job, completed at least a four year college degree, secured a good position, and continued being there for my family, if needed.

Life can be this way: You start acquiring things like bills (debt). You need money to pay bills. So you work. And you keep working. You have a family. You have responsibilities. And you keep working. You have to pay utilities and you have to eat. You keep working. You and your children have to be clothed and you need a place to live. You keep working. Okay. But guess what? It is a little bit easier when you have more income because you have more knowledge.

If you are over forty years of age, you may have heard the stories where someone was passed up for a promotion they were surely qualified for because they had been with the company for years and could perform the tasks of the position without blinking an eye. But the next step up as supervisor, or assistant vice president (or whatever the title) required that "piece of paper." And even though you apply, you keep getting passed up. Now you're in night school finishing up your degree because you're tired of telling your wife or husband why you didn't get the job. The kids are getting older, and a couple of the children will be going to college in a few years. You want to be there for them financially during that time if they need you. Now you have to juggle work, school, and family. If you haven't got to this point in life, do me a favor. Don't do this backwards. Do everything in your power (especially if you plan on working corporate or for someone else) to complete your college education. Get that diploma. You never know when you will need specified knowledge to have an advantage for further opportunity in your career. Do not have this door shut in your face.

A few decades ago it was sufficient, in many occupations, for a candidate to possess only vocational certificates of completion, but nowadays, a four year college degree is required in most fields, and a good number of corporations want you to have a bachelor's degree just to hold the title of receptionist, or even department secretary. Companies feel they are better represented if you have a formal university education. And no matter how well-spoken you are, no matter how articulate, no matter how you enunciate your words, your completed degree is the industry's comfort in knowing you qualify. Self-educated or not. Four classes shy of completing your degree means nothing. Either you have it, or you don't. The hiring manager does not want to hear stories or reasons. They only want to see completed results – your college degree. You want to know something else? For certain professions (to even get your foot in the door) they want to know what your grade point average is. That's right. I kid you not. So if you want to work for ABC/ XYZ Company, and you see yourself working on the penthouse floor of the firm within 10 years or less – you better know what's up before you finish college. Hell, know what's up before you start college. And if you can, intern for them (or the like) before graduating. Have something on your résumé along the line of your chosen occupation before you complete your studies. And if you are hired with a company in your field of choice, count your blessings, then prepare to work hard. Dues have to be paid. Dues are: *time; discipline; hard work; accountability; professionalism; dependability; reliability; further knowledge; doing what it takes to get the job done; being punctual; overtime may be required; no whining; diligence; desire; a healthy body; a healthy and sharp mind*, and most of all....with all this....sometimes *patience*.

PATIENCE. What is patience? Doing something without complaining, right? Diligence. Persevering. Enduring. Calmly tolerating (if it gets to this point). Yes?

My definition of patience is doing what it takes until the results are achieved to the end in which you desire of what you intend to accomplish *without complaining.*

Furthermore, after you had patience, and did all you could, and put everything in place (and in motion) to achieve the end in which you desire for your intended accomplishment---you may have to have even **more patience** and wait on someone else to complete their part to get the **true** **end** **results** or to realize the **actual** intended outcome. I know this much. If you deal with sales (especially real estate) you have been there many of times. So do not act like you don't know what I am talking about. Whether you are the selling agent, the buying agent, a part of the escrow staff, a part of the title staff, or a part of the lending staff. Whether you are the seller of the property, or the buyer......do not act as if you don't know what I am talking about. And if you are an existing homeowner, trying to get a loan on your property, or a modification on your loan, I know you are familiar with what I am saying here. If you are married – you have patience *for real*!! (Snap your fingers two times if you are married and you need patience). If you have children, I know you have patience (at least you should). (Snap your fingers three times if you have a teenager). Yep! Patience. You are probably laughing right now, but again, I am very serious.

Patience is a virtue. Patience is a necessary quality to have in this day of living. The understanding of patience, and why it is important to exercise patience when necessary, helps reduce stress levels in your body and can actually keep stress to a bare minimum. Stress is very dangerous. Your body does not like stress. Stress can be detrimental to your health.

ASSIGNMENT: Google stress and how it affects the body. Pay close attention to the signs of stress, especially when it comes to your heart.

Did you do it? Are you highly stressed already? Do you need stress management? If so, seek stress management assistance. Please Google and locate companies, institutions, or organizations that assist with stress management in your area. And while you are at it, have your blood pressure checked as soon as possible. Thank you.

You know it is important to be fit/healthy to work – to be employed, right? I think it is also important to be healthy and physically fit (as best as possible) while you are attending school (middle school, high school, college, etc.). It is important to be healthy mentally and physically, period.

We are about achieving our best so....now I'm coming with what do you know about your body? I did not even know I was sick before my surgery. I thought I just had a frequent case of indigestion and acid reflux, but I had a bleeding ulcer and a cancerous tumor in my stomach. I didn't feel very sick. I sure did not look sick. My eating pattern changed. But what did I do? I contributed it all to stress. I was *actually* walking around *dying* and I did not know it. So yeah, I am about to get in your business. I don't want something this serious to happen to you. I care.

What do you know about your body? When was the last time you had a complete physical exam? When was the last time you had a dental exam? When was the last time you had a complete and thorough examination of your eyes? Did you know that if you go for extended periods of time without having your teeth and gums cleaned properly it can trigger other problems in your body?

ASSIGNMENT: Google/research gum disease and how it can affect the body (particularly the stomach).

Do you know what your BMI is (body mass index)? Are you anywhere near that number?

Is your body toned? Or do you shake like jello when you move? I don't know about you but the lower part of my behind is trying to socialize with the back part of my upper thighs. They are getting too damn close, and it seems like my ass wants to have a conversation with my thighs, and if my body parts could talk it would go like this:

Ass: What's up thighs?

Thighs: *Apparently,* not you.

See what I'm saying? I gotta do something about that. It is time for a sister to get toned and fit again. Squats, leg lifts---you know the drill.

I am serious about my thighs and behind. Even though I am petite, I still have to tone up. I am usually physically fit, but I haven't really worked out this year. And now it is August, 2014. I started writing this book in June. I stopped writing for a bit (for about six weeks), but today is August 11, 2014, and I intend to have this book finished by the end of September, 2014. My birthday is September 2, and I will not even stop writing on that day.

Back to your body. Do you have a regular exercise routine? How is your cardio activity? Do you look the way you would like to look? If so, great! If not, do something about it.

Make sure you get a physical examination of your body prior to getting involved in a workout program. Make sure your body (*especially your heart*) is fit to endure what you plan for a workout routine.

If you belong to a health club, know the proper use of the exercise equipment. You should have had a complete tour of the club facilities. Have someone demonstrate proper use of **every** piece of equipment intended for your workout routine. Before I had my son, I worked for a popular health club part-time. I was amazed at how many people did not know how to use the gym equipment **correctly**, or were even able to perform proper aerobic techniques (in a *high impact* aerobics class). I am a hands on person. I would demonstrate use of the machines when it was necessary to do so, and when instructing the high impact aerobics class, I would come down from the podium and assist members *individually* with technique, form, and posture to ensure they were getting the best benefit and achieving the results they desired from the class. You don't want injuries in the process of getting in shape. The club should have team members to assist you. Don't be shy. If you need help – ask.

If the health club has personal trainers on site, take advantage of this service. Sometimes you will get a couple of free sessions. *A personal trainer is a plus.* Keep one as long as you can afford it. It is best to work with a trainer at least three times a week. Starting off, work with a trainer for no less than six months. Find a way to afford it because proper use of equipment and how the equipment benefits the body is important to know. Also, and most importantly, trainers will hold you accountable to your personal fitness program. You have to set appointments with your trainer, and you should keep the appointment with your trainer. Exercise programs at home are fine, but you don't have to turn that on when you don't feel like it, and, at home, only **you** will know when you're exercising or not. You need accountability. You need to be healthy all of your days, and God willing, you will live for a good while. Know what you are doing when it comes to exercise and your body.

You don't want to belong to a health club/gym right now? Enjoy the outdoors. Go for nice 30 minute walks – everyday. Work your way up to an hour. Join a walking club. Ask your neighbor to walk with you. Walking is fun and enjoying the outdoors is refreshing. You can walk at a park or a local high school. **Carefully** go up and down the bleachers on the field for an extra workout. You burn a lot of calories walking those bleachers. (Psst: When I used to run the bleachers my legs were sooo sexxxy and toned).

These are not for you? How about dancing? In Los Angeles, California we have Lula Washington dance studios on Crenshaw Boulevard, and we have Debbie Allen's dance studio in the

Crenshaw district. Both are excellent choices. You can take Hip Hop, Jazz, Tap, and Ballet. Lula Washington, and Debbie Allen offer other types of dancing you would enjoy also. Look them up on the internet. There is something for the entire family in dance. I studied modern dance three years straight in high school. The experience is beautiful. The body feels so good after dancing. You feel your *entire* being in the moves. The rhythm of the music seems to connect with your heart and mind. You immerse yourself in the experience. Every time is different. You forget the rest of the day when you move to the beat. Even if it's just the beat and rhythm of your heart you hear when you're dancing – nothing else matters. Your body and mind feel so light. No matter how fast you're moving – no matter how slow you're moving. The feeling is amazing. And when you perform dance, you get to share that experience with others and it brings delight. Oh, I'm sorry. I took myself back for a minute. I plan to join a dance studio soon. I have cousins that attended both Lula Washington and Debbie Allen's dance studios. I subscribe to Dance Magazine I love dance so much. I also plan to take up shadow boxing for exercise. There is a shadow boxing studio on Beverly Boulevard in Los Angeles about 10 minutes from the Beverly Center. I'm going to check and see if it is still there.

If you have to lose weight, I know this can be a challenge. A couple of times as an adult I was at least 50 pounds more than what I should weigh for my 5'4" body. Try to, as much as possible, be mindful of your weight. Make sure you incorporate a workout routine in your weekly schedule - and stick to it. Sometimes this can be a challenge within itself.

Make sure your body is properly nourished, and drink plenty of water. As you know, the human body is almost 70% water. To maintain good health, it is important to consume about 2 to 2 ½ half quarts of water daily through drinking and eating (especially when you are exercising regularly). Water helps to *regulate* your body's temperature.

ASSIGNMENT: Google the health benefits of the Aloe Vera Plant. Google the health benefits of Vitamin C.

ASSIGNMENT: Google the health benefits of strawberries, bananas, apples, kale, collard greens, turnip greens, carrots, celery, garlic, and cucumbers.

I focus on eating right daily. I take ¼ cup of Aloe Vera juice every night before I go to sleep. I take 1000mg of vitamin C in the morning and another 1000mg of vitamin C in the evening. I take 1000**mcg** of the B12 vitamin a day, and I take two of GNC's Women's Hair, Skin & Nails Formula vitamin a day.

I hope you're looking these assignments up if you don't know what they're about already. This should be helpful.

What are you thinking? What is going on in your mind?

Do you try to make a habit of thinking positive thoughts? It seems to be easy to get off course and think negative, doesn't it? You know how they say, "You are what you think about?" Have you noticed when you put a lot of emphasis on what is negative, or wrong, or bad, it seems to come to pass faster than anything else you think of? Truth is, what you put the most *e-m-o-t-i-o-n* into usually comes to fruition first. Would you agree? Think about it. Think about what comes through first when it comes to your positive and negative thoughts. Where are you placing most of your emotion? Am I right?

Those so-called "bad days" you have at work. Are they really "bad days," or are you habitually thinking about stuff that's not so good *d-a-i-l-y*? If you work full-time, that is a big chunk of your life. How productive are you when you are working? Do you have to cram in the majority of your work in the 2 ½ to 3 remaining hours of the workday because of where your mind was the majority of the day? If you do, how effective are you, and what is the quality of your work? You want a raise in salary or a promotion, don't you? If this is you – guess what? You are not getting the raise or the promotion if you continue in this manner. If this is you, what is causing you to think this way? Your home life? Your love life (or lack thereof)? Concerned about your children? Don't have any children? Your appearance? Your debt? The car you drive? What's wrong with your car? You need a car? Your wardrobe? You want more savings? You want to go on a nice vacation? Something else happened that makes life not so good right now? Do you like where you live? You would like to change jobs but don't know what to do right now? Having another birthday and feeling a little melancholy because you haven't accomplished your goals, or haven't found the one you want to love forever yet?

Ninety five percent of what I said in the above paragraph I have already experienced. See, this is why we are one-on-one right now.

What we think are "bad days" are not as bad as they seem. Yes, it could be worse because you don't have to be alive to experience the day. And please, don't say I wish I wasn't alive to experience the day. If you feel this way, then you just haven't thought of enough reasons to want to experience the day. How you think and feel does affect how you work, how you live, how you love, *and how you allow yourself to be loved.*

I pray that you are happy. I pray that you already have joy upon joy in your life. I pray that you have that special person or those special people in your life already. I pray that you don't have money problems, or debt you think you see no end to. I pray that you have peace in your soul. I pray that you are healthy. I pray that you know how to love. I pray that you have the knowledge to have understanding for everything that is good and sometimes not so good in your life. I pray that you have a belief system that keeps you focused. I pray, most of all, that you can be you. That you can be who you were born to be. I pray that you have that peace within yourself if you have nothing else. I pray this. *Psalm 20:4, "May He grant you according to your heart's desire, and fulfill all your purpose."*

I don't know you personally yet, but if you are reading this book, you must be very special and you were put here for a purpose, and that purpose - you *shall* have.

If, at the moment, you don't have what you want, or that happiness within---you will. You will be content, and you will learn how to have and experience peace. You will get that in this reading. When that light comes on, and that one thing clicks in – it sinks in.....you'll know it. You might cry. You might scream. Your body might just shake. Your hands may tremble. You may feel a coolness over your body. You may sweat. You may become angry. You might just want go outside and run down the street. Be careful of traffic though if you do. But baby....it's right here.....it's right here. I got you. You believe in something. I know you do. I feel it. Whatever it is, hold on to it. Because in the end you will not be disappointed.

We have to stay **focused**. We have to stay **productive**. We all need a **purpose**. You don't want to just wander around. If you are wandering around---STOP IT!!! Find something to hold onto.

I find happiness, joy, and peace in many things. Here is where I find happiness and peace:

I love the sound of the wind blowing in the trees.

I love stepping on dried leaves in the fall and winter.

I love the smell of the outdoors after a good rain. I love the sound of rain.

I love the laughter of children. It makes me smile to see children learning and being educated.

I love looking at the ocean and watching the waves in the water.

I love a clear blue sky, and I love fluffy white clouds.

I love to hear the choir singing in the church.

I love to take relaxing walks.

I love the sound of my son's laughter. I love the sound of his wife Melissa's voice.

You see, everything I mentioned above is free. Happiness doesn't have to cost you a fortune. You don't have to be wealthy *financially* to be happy.

But, since everything is not free. Back to business. So dry those eyes, and let's keep going.

Your brain is a very important part of you. Use it wisely.

On the subject of the brain, let's get into brain waves for a minute. Alpha, Beta, Theta, and Delta.

ALPHA: When we are in a state of physical relaxation, and at the same time, aware of what is happening around us.

BETA: Emitted when we are consciously alert or feel agitated, tense, and sometimes afraid.

THETA: When we are in a state of somnolence (drowsiness/ sleepy) with reduced consciousness.

DELTA: When there is unconsciousness (deep sleep).

We stay in the Beta rhythm more than we should. When the brain is in Alpha, we are in the ideal condition to learn new information and perform elaborate tasks. In the Alpha wave, we are in an optimum state of thinking to keep facts and data better, and have the ability to better analyze complex situations. A couple of ways to get the brain to the Alpha state is through meditation and relaxation exercises and activities. Here you experience a sense of calm. We want to be in the Alpha state as much as possible.

ASSIGNMENT: Google brain wave therapy.

ASSIGNMENT: Google and study Metaphysics for a little bit. This branch of philosophy touches on subjects such as determinism and free will. You will also learn a bit about identity and change, and mind and matter. This is a very interesting read. If you don't know about metaphysics already you should find it very fascinating.

It is important to know how people think and come to conclusions about certain topics such as belief systems, and how the universe serves us, and how we as humans can view *the same information differently*. This can, obviously, affect how we interact with one another, how we work together, as well as, how we socialize with each other.

TWO

NEGATIVES AND POSITIVES

Whether you are self-employed, or you work for someone else, it is important to have extensive knowledge of your occupation.

Research the position you are seeking before you attempt to get hired for the job. Know, at least, what the median income is for the position, and be able to be "*that person*" in every way, form, and fashion. Know that you deserve to get paid what you are worth. Look at it this way, if you were on the hiring side, and it was your company, what skills should the person possess for that particular position? What talent, what character, who would be your ideal candidate? This is who you need to be if you want to get hired. Period. This is who you <u>should</u> be <u>before</u> walking in the door.

Once hired, be accountable. Do not become settled and comfortable, and "chummy", and acquainted with everyone and start taking your job lightly, and for granted. In the early twenty first century (even as of the year 2014), jobs are hard to come by, so don't start taking away from yourself (or the company) once you pass the probationary period of being hired. Too *many* employees make unnecessary mistakes – then begin to wonder what happened when it is all over.

Here are some serious mistakes: You start coming in a few minutes later. You go to <u>break early</u>, or come back from <u>break later</u> than you should. You leave a few minutes early. Your quality of work *isn't superior*. You began slacking in your position and **you don't** care because you think you're "in." You are able to complete your assignments for the day, and still have a considerable amount of time left before the completion of the workday. **You don't** ask anyone else on your team [or in your department] if assistance is needed to finish necessary work for the company to *keep production levels up*. **You don't** ask to be cross-trained on another desk so you'll have work to do *throughout the entire workday*. Cross-training is usually necessary for a company so that the flow of work remains steady should someone call in sick, <u>really</u> need to leave early, or have a legitimate reason for coming in late. This helps the company *stay* strong. Many companies work with deadlines that cannot be missed, and *knowledgeable* employees have to fulfill certain tasks. Instead of trying to know what **you don't** have to do because it's "not *your* job," **apply yourself** and desire to be that "go to" person (focus on that). The company you work for should easily be able to see that you are not there just for a paycheck. You want to make it apparent that you are there for the company, you want to be a part of the company, and you want to be a part of the growth of the company. Your employer should know that you care about where you work, just like you want them to care about you. If this doesn't apply to you, and you know what's up, then you already have understanding. If this does apply to you, and none of this is registering in your brain at the moment, then look at it from this perspective---if this was your company and you started it from the ground up, wouldn't you want staff that cared as much for the business as you do? Would you want someone stealing from you? Yes, stealing! So, if the company automatically does not pay when you come in late or leave early, etcetera, etc., then this is not applicable to you. But if you are an exempt employee, you are taking from the company. Just add up all of the time you have come in late, left early, and took long (unproductive lunches). Add this information up for the complete time you have worked for the firm so far. Based on your annual salary, what does that number come to?

Were you contributing to the firm when you were away from the office in a way that would create growth and development for the company? Well, were you? And then people wonder why that dreadful meeting of "we regret to inform you that our doors will be closing permanently in "X" amount of days" eventually comes. I don't care how large an organization is - there is always room for growth and development. The business development side of any organization is an extremely urgent part of the company's existence. Companies have to stay on top of their game, or they will end up at the bottom. This is why it is key to hire and add members to staff who would actually care about the future of the company, and be on board with what the company represents. You want to feel good when you go to work, and you should work for a company that you can actually be proud of. Don't work for a company that you don't feel good about or you could not truly say you are proud to be in their employment. If you do this, you are making yourself miserable, and wasting your employer's time. Do not deceive the company. When you are asked questions in the hiring interview, be honest with your answers. The company wants to know what you are about, and you have the opportunity to know what they are about as well. Use this opportunity wisely, or you will have regrets later. Regrets equal coming in late, longer breaks, etc., etc. If I hired a person like this, I would eventually begin to think that individual no longer wanted their job.

The company you work for deserves the best, and you deserve the best as a person.

You should desire to be happy, and desire to perform at your optimum ability as much as possible.

If you are unhappy, it is imperative for you to know what is causing you to feel this way. You may have started out on the "right foot" with that job, or even with your own business, but in the process, something may have happened – causing a change for the worst. What is that something? You have to find out what it is before it is too late. Don't let this destroy the business you built, or let this take away your ability to remain employed with the company you decided to join. Do not become lost in this circle of emotions. Do not let whatever this is take you away from being your best, and from being who you should be. This, whatever it is, cannot be bigger than you. This "thing" cannot be that bad where you lose complete focus and throw everything away, or can't even start what you really want in the first place. Don't allow this to take over your brain where you cannot thrive or live in content and peace. If you are discontent about anything at this time, you have to sort through your emotions and find out what it is. If you have undesired mood changes, when does this occur? What causes your emotions to fluctuate in a direction you do not want? Can you change this? Is someone else or something else involved? How so? Is it something someone is doing, or something that they are saying to you? When does this happen? Why does it happen? What triggers it? When it happens, how long does it last? What are your actual emotions when this takes place, and what is your body language like at this time? Does this spill over into your work or your personal life outside of work? Most importantly, **can you control it?**

You have to have these answers as soon as possible. Every time you get an answer **write it down.** If this is something that is going on currently, you cannot run away from it, you have to acknowledge this to go forward.

When I find myself in this state of being (and it has happened), I regroup, and as painful sometimes as it can be, recollect and refocus, and I do this now as fast as possible. The unfortunate thing is, sometimes damage has already been done before you are aware that something **needs to be done** in order to come out of it. You find yourself in a fog. No need to be ashamed though. It happens to many people. And don't even be ashamed if it took you a little longer to realize it. As the saying goes, "Better late than never." And if someone else was indirectly (but somehow directly) affected by what you went through, well…all you can do is sincerely apologize, then let that person know that you are going to do everything you can to correct the situation, and that you will care, and if love is involved, you will love in the process of this transition. Ask this person to have patience and trust in you. Give it <u>your all</u>, and let go and let God, because this may be big and you might need a little help. It **will** be okay. In the Bible, in the *First Epistle of Peter, 5:6-7 it says, "Therefore humble yourselves under the mighty hand of God that He may exalt you in due time, casting all your care upon Him, for He cares for you."*

Once I realize what is really going on, and have completely assessed the situation I am dealing with, I like to keep my mood as light as possible. One way I do this is through being entertained with comedy. I am still fully aware of what is going on in my life, but I feel that being down about it is not going to make it better. During the process of being focused and aware, I keep my mood light.

I love to laugh. Making people laugh naturally is not always easy. When I was in the hospital for the bleeding ulcer and for the gastrectomy, I watched Steve Harvey almost every day. I was at the Good Samaritan Hospital for eleven days. The doctors commented numerous times on how well I was recovering. Keep in mind, the bleeding ulcer would have taken my life had another week past, and at the same time, I found out I had stage three stomach cancer. Other than being in the hospital for having a baby twenty eight years ago, I had never been hospitalized for anything. Is that heavy or what? Like Gladys Knight says, "You've got to make the best of a bad situation and keep on keepin' on." I watched so much comedy in the hospital I remember waking up a few times laughing from the dreams I was having. Word of advice though, wait at least two months after any surgery before watching Saturday Night Live. I probably did some internal damage at home from laughing so hard while watching this show. So I waited another month after surgery before watching the program again. I have been watching Saturday Night Live since high school. I should have known better.

I want to take this time to thank all of the comedians of the world and the entertainers who make me laugh. You do not know how special you are and how much *you are truly appreciated.* A special thank you to: Bill Cosby, Richard Pryor, Redd Foxx, Steve Harvey, Bernie Mac, Cedric the Entertainer, D.L. Hughley, Martin Lawrence, Robin Williams, Goldie Hawn, Whoopi Goldberg, Steve Martin, Eddie Murphy, Katt Williams, Chris Tucker, Seth Meyers, Jimmy Fallon, Chris Rock, Jay Leno, The entire Wayans family, Jimmy Walker, The entire cast, writers, and producers of Ugly Betty, the entire cast, writers, and producers of The Cosby Show, Jim Carey, the entire cast, writers, and producers of the Fresh Prince of Bel Air, Tracy Morgan, Roseanne, Ellen DeGeneres, Joan Rivers, Conan O'Brien (he makes me laugh), Ice Cube (when he's doing comedy in a movie), Mike Epps, Jimmy Kimmel, everyone that performed/performs on Saturday Night Live, the entire cast, writers, and producers of In Living Color, Lucille Ball, Jerry Lewis, Robin Harris, my cousin Michael Williams from Los Angeles and his comedy clubs- Comedy Act Theater, and Jamie Foxx. You are all priceless.

I love comedy shows. I love comedy movies. And yes, I go to the theater and watch animated movies where the audience is usually twelve years old and younger accompanied by adults. And no, I don't have a child with me at the time. And if you're thinking it, of course I still watch the Simpsons! Laughter is very therapeutic. *Proverbs 17:22 says, "A merry heart does good, like medicine, but a broken spirit dries the bones."*

I am starting from the inside of the body (our health, our mind, our feelings) because it matters. It is clearly obvious this complete package encompasses you as a person – *who you are*. What you think <u>affects</u> your <u>every</u> outcome. A lot of what you think and what is given to you as information has the meaning <u>you</u> place on it.

For instance, the following are a couple of advertisement examples.

Let's say I am placing an ad in a magazine that, well...*maybe all family members <u>should not read</u>*. And the ad goes like this....

Ummm. This is the perfect LENGTH and the perfect WIDTH. Ummm...I love wrapping my fingers around it. *I have skills.* I am sure he'll appreciate this and love that I did it. UMMM. Hot enough/spicy...oh, a little salty too! **Tonight** *is a good night.*

What do you think I am talking about?

Okay, turn the page in your mind. The next page shows you a picture of a cracker with lightly melted cheese, a couple of kalamato olives, and a little bit of chopped serrano chile (no seeds). See what I mean? Our own interpretation. I am just talking about a mouth-watering appetizer.

The next ad is placed in a **classy/high profile magazine** – geared toward success and **for the accomplished.** The entire page is all gold/slick, and shiny – the words are bold and beautifully written. The ad goes like this:

ELEGANT. EXCEPTIONAL. EXTRAORDINARY.

The best watch you will ever own is waiting for you. Go to one of these fine stores and try it on today.

No picture of the watch is shown. The name of the watch and the maker of the watch is mentioned. A list of about five stores where the average wrist watch starts at $25,000 U.S dollars is featured. I bet you show up!

It is true that we oftentimes place our "*little special meaning*" on most of what we mentally internalize. This can be catastrophic to our careers.

This was one of my biggest obstacles in my professional career as a real estate agent. I allowed this to stop me many a times, right in my tracks on the road to success. What was said to me and *what I let it mean.* I noticed this pattern almost twenty years ago, but couldn't shake myself from it. Mainly because it came from people who should love me and care. People that are close to me. I am certain these feelings from some of these individuals were already in place, I just didn't want to own up to it as young as 18 and 19 years old. Even some of my friends noticed and mentioned it. My friends noticed my haters. It is the feeling of envy and hate. And it hurts. These type of feelings from others progressed when I began a career in real estate. In real estate, I had the opportunity to have and be more for myself, to grow and develop as a person, and surely, to write my own ticket to success. The sky could be the limit with hard work.

It was sad because I would work hard---make a few sales--accomplish my short-term goals and have immediate (short-term) success. This work behavior became a pattern for me. The haters noticed my ability to make a decent income. Then they would make comments---comments to bring me down. Apparently they didn't want to see me soar and rise to the destination I had for myself, <u>and I allowed it</u> by *internalizing* their negative words.

This is hurtful because someone you have deep feelings for and care about is bringing you down. I dated a high school teacher for a while – one who apparently did not want to see me successful. In 2003 I joined the Spectrum Club, he said, "Why would you want to belong to <u>that</u> health club?" I said, "I want to buy a Range Rover," he said, "Why would you want to buy *that* kind of car?" And every time I mentioned anything remotely close to a resemblance of success, he had a negative comment to make. I should have left him alone then because he did not have my best interest at heart. I should have realized one thing at that time if I did not realize anything else, and it is this: if he did not want to see me so much as desire better *for myself*, then certainly he would not offer me better *from himself*. That is not love. That is envy and hate. I guess a person can be intimate with you and date you, and at the same time display these negative emotions for you. He made it no secret. I dated him three years longer than I should have. The relationship ended March, 2007. This kind of person is someone who does not have good intentions for you, does not want to see you with anyone who does, and probably hopes you're stupid enough to not realize *you can* have anything good you want. This kind of person can be toxic to your system. Dating can be that way sometimes - keep your eyes open.

Then you have the judgmental folks. These are people who are never really happy and *I think they live this way on purpose*. They look for things to find fault in, and if there is nothing there, they create it. You cannot please them <u>ever</u>, so don't try. These are the folks who, many a times, will go to church to be the judge. They are loquacious, and they send negative energy down the entire pew they're sitting in. They will pass the collection plate, and won't put anything in it. And after all of that, have the audacity to stay for the next service. If you ever sat on a row like this at church, say amen. If this book was being read universally, simultaneously, I bet that would have been a resounding amen. It is in every church. No matter how small the church, no matter how large the congregation---it is present. I will say what a lot of pastors won't. It needs to stop <u>now</u>. You're sitting up there talking about, "Didn't he/she preach that same sermon two weeks ago?" Did you prepare a message? Maybe the pastor wouldn't mind if you came up one day and preached since you have so much to say. Pastors work hard to bring the message across in a way that you can understand *and* benefit. There is only one real judge. I don't think that's us. The Bible is an interesting book, and as old as it is, people are still the same if you read it right. There are only so many personalities in this world. And the saying holds true "same thing, different date." Pastors are not perfect. Unless you have a robot in your pulpit, know that they are not perfect and they do sin. And robots malfunction – so don't even go there. To quote Alexander Pope, "To err is human; to forgive, divine." People who judge in a negative critical way are undercover haters in my book. Down-low haters. Low-low haters. Haters were not born yesterday, they have been around for centuries, and yes, there are generations of haters. So don't think you're special with your little song that "everybody hates me, oh, woe is me. Why they trippin' on me? I'm just trying to come up." Unless you're sitting around watching the grass grow, you might have a few haters here and there in your lifetime. Know how to deal with it. If you intend on being successful at <u>anything,</u> you might have a hater or two. It is inevitable. Whether you pastor a church, or own a bank – if your mission is to be successful, everyone may not agree with your entire program. So watch out for your frenemies. You may have a business venture, or a church that may increase in size. Is this not the intention? Whatever your mission – you want to reach your goal. This level of increase may be an abundance. As you help and bless others, God will help and bless you. You give, and you will receive. Whatever your business, if someone is open to what you are giving, then you will receive – it is as simple as that. You paint and sell one portrait – you sell many portraits. You have a church of 100 members – your flock grows. Now more people want to hear how Y-O-U deliver God's message – so now you have a larger congregation. You design one dress – it sells – you sell more dresses. You have one grocery store, now you have a chain of grocery stores. This is what the Bible calls increase. God did not put you here to live in poverty. You are here to live a *happy* and *abundant* life. Strive for that, and in the process don't envy or hate someone who has been successful in their mission in life. It is not healthy, and your negative attitude toward others is actually stifling. *Proverbs 14:23, "In all labor there is profit, but idle chatter leads only to poverty."* Green looks good on emeralds – not on you.

EVERYONE HAS THIS ASSIGNMENT: Google and read the **entire** poem "Essay on Criticism" by Alexander Pope.

It is important that you understand this poem as much as possible – every stanza. It might help you. It may liberate you. Alexander Pope was born in 1688. Yes, people can be the same. Same thing, different date, unfortunately. The poem is beautiful, yet true. Read it and "mentally digest" it.

The "Essay on Criticism" says, "Not free from faults, nor yet too vain to mend."

Book of Romans 12:18 says, "If it is possible, as much as depends on you, live peaceably with all men."

Romans 14, 12-13: "So then each of us shall give account of himself to God. Therefore let us not judge one another anymore, but rather resolve this, not to put a stumbling block or a cause to fall in our brother's way."

Romans 14:19, "Therefore let us pursue the things which make for peace and the things by which one may edify another."

See, sometimes you may have to go back a little to understand where you are today in your thinking. How much have you taken in from others - no matter the method of communication – verbal, written, text, etc. – that you may have possibly misconstrued? Your thinking might make a difference in where you are today.

If your mind is in bondage free it so you can progress in life. <u>Live in power</u>. <u>Live in peace</u>.

THREE

DON'T GET CAUGHT UP

A healthy mental capacity is necessary to be self-sufficient. We know this. You have to stay as strong as possible mentally and physically because you never know when the mind or the body has to take over and compensate for the other.

After surgery, I was very physically weak. I usually carry a larger-sized handbag. I couldn't even lift it. I needed help getting up to go to the rest room. I felt very physically drained. A feeling I never felt before, but **my mind was strong** – my thoughts were very much in place and I was still **extremely mentally focused**.

I kept telling myself I had to survive and death was not an option. That day was March 17, my son was getting married to his college sweetheart on June 7. I would be there for that wedding. I stayed focused. I began to feel no pain from my surgery in just a matter of a few days. I would not let those feelings register. **I focused on feeling good. I focused on my future**.

I had already ordered the continuing education courses for my real estate license renewal the week before I became very sick. The absolute deadline to renew my four year license was April

21. I was released from the hospital on March 27. A few days after, I began studying the continuing education courses: *Risk Management*, *Fair Housing*, *Ethics*, *Agency Relationships*, *Trust Fund Handling*, *Healthy Homes*, and *Property Management* (sections one and two). I scored high in all subjects. I completed all courses the day before the deadline and renewed my license online – on time! It was a lot of reading, but *my mind was sharp*. I could barely walk up the stairs in my friend Cidney Walker's home to take a shower - I had to hold on to the handrails and walk *real* slow, but *my mind was sharp*!! My friend Cidney has been an RN since 2002. She gave me a bath the first day I left the hospital. I was able to bathe myself the next day. I was still weak, but *my mind was strong*. I did not have the physical strength to open my own medicine bottles, but *I was focused mentally*! I kept telling myself I was physically strong and capable – I could do this. In less than a week from leaving the hospital I was walking around Walmart shopping. Now I am *physically and mentally strong*. I had a bleeding ulcer removed, my stomach removed, and a hernia removed. I was a little sore, but my mind was *strong and fit*! I did not have to have chemotherapy or radiation. I am going to continue to believe I will stay healed.

I would like to quote Psalm 28: 8-9, *"The Lord is their strength, and He is the saving refuge of His anointed. Save Your people, and bless Your inheritance; Shepherd them also, and bear them up forever."*

Proverbs 16:9 says, *"A man's heart plans his way, but the Lord directs his steps."*

Always pray for strength and health. Pray and believe this at all times whether you are sick or not. Pray this everyday of your life. I do. Today is September 1, tomorrow I will be 53 years old, and right now – unless God takes me – death is not an option. I still have things to do and something I want to say. I started writing this book less than three months after having surgery. I will complete this book in September, 2014.

As I mentioned earlier, it is important to take the best care possible of yourself <u>always</u>, mentally and physically, and the sooner you start - the better, amen! *Always strive to look and be your best*, because even when you don't feel your best – you can look alright.

Some products I use are old regimens, and some things are new. For instance. I have used Palmer's Cocoa Butter products since I was thirteen years old. I have used Olay Active Hydrating Beauty Fluid Lotion (original formula) on my face since I was twenty three years old. I have used St. Ives Apricot Scrub on my face since I was twenty three years old. I began using Olay facial wipes, Olay Foaming Face Wash, and Olay Oil Minimizing Toner in my late thirties, and I started using Olay's eye revitalizing eye gel in my early forties. After I got out of the hospital, my face looked dry so I chose to use Palmer's Cocoa Butter Formula Night Renewal Cream. I use Palmer's Night Renewal Cream because it does what it says it's going to do. It's as simple as that. To minimize the appearance of my surgical incision and staple marks (which are barely visible now) I use Bio-Oil (bio-oilusa.com). Bio-Oil is an excellent product. When I wash my face, I start with warm water, then final rinse with very cold water. I wash my face in an upward motion, and apply facial products in the same upward motion manner.

I believe that skin should be as naturally beautiful as possible, and make-up minimal. Make-up, in my opinion, should be used to accent your beauty and change/highlight your facial features *if you want*. Make-up, again, in my opinion, should not be used to cover up. If you have constant skin problems you may want to seek the help of a dermatologist, because when the make-up comes off - those problem areas are still there.

For my skin, I love the True Blue Spa line. The bar soap cleanses well and it is very rich and creamy. I especially love True Blue Spa's Pineapple Papaya Nourishing Yogurt Shower Smoothie – this is very good. And their Shea Butter Fresh Foaming Body Buff is also excellent. My skin is <u>always</u> very soft. You can buy True Blue Spa products from Bath and Body Works.

For my diet, I try to eat healthy. My system is "hooked up" like someone who has had a gastric bypass surgery, so I can still eat most foods. I just have to refrain from eating very sweet and sugary foods because I have no stomach to break down certain elements sugars have. I can eat Lorna Doone Shortbread cookies with no problem, and I can eat the cheese cake from Maria's Italian Kitchen with no problem. I have to chew my food very well, eat at least eight small meals a day, and drink beverages at least 30-45 minutes <u>after</u> I eat. I like to add Crystal Light Peach-Mango Green Tea to my water. I drink a lot of water.

I am gaining my weight back very well. I eat foods that don't irritate my body or make me very "gassy". I enjoy eating the food from Seasalt Fishgrill on 7th and Figueroa in Downtown Los Angeles. I usually order the salmon off the grill cooked Cajun style served with vegetables and rice. I go to Seasalt Fishgrill at least 2-3 times a week and am considered a VIP customer because of my frequent visits. You should check them out – I highly recommend them. Try to avoid their lunch hour rush (the place is *busy*). Seasalt's website address is www.seasaltfishgrill.com. They take phone orders and also cater. Another good restaurant tip is Maria's Italian Kitchen. The lasagna and the Boulevard Pizza are **very** delicious. Maria's food doesn't bother my digestive system (mariasitaliankitchen.com). I eat a lot of protein, a good amount of rice, and a good amount of starch (carbs). I usually have two eggs (protein), and an English muffin every day.

Mr. Philip Whitley Lankford of Simply Raw Hair Designs in Los Angeles has been doing my hair since the summer of 2011. Philip is an excellent stylist and no one could pay me to leave him. Philip's work is amazing.

A good tip for women: If you don't use satin pillow cases, *sleep with a satin scarf on your head.* Cotton pillow cases can dry the hair and may cause hair breakage.

Also, exercise to keep your body strong and your lungs healthy.

Why am I telling you this personal information? Because most people don't. They want you to think they were born that way and never changed.

People often tell me I look like I'm in my thirties, and men in my age group rarely flirt with me because they think I am a lot younger. More often than not, I have guys hitting on me that are about 30-35 years old, and when my son and I go to lunch, he says, "Mom, how come the waiter always gives me the check?" Seriously!

I have never had cosmetic surgery and I don't use Botox. There is nothing wrong with cosmetic surgery or Botox, I just don't use them.

Men and women, start young with your health and beauty regimen – don't wait until you turn 40. Men: I bet you wish there was Olay for men? Or, am I late? It might already be on the market. Even after surgery and after near death, people still thought I looked much younger than what I was – 52. I don't have any wrinkles in my face, and I have very few gray hairs.

You especially want to look good when trying times come your way. You don't want to look like the hell you are going through. Unless you tell, no one needs to know about your personal *momentary* battles except you. So don't advertise it with the look on your face. My mother told me at a young age, when you are going through your worst – you should try to look your best.

Speaking of some of the worst times. I remember when real estate was taking a turn *for the worst.* Who could forget? It touched a lot of people. I worked with Re/Max Real Estate Specialists from 1997 until 2008 – a very fine real estate company. Anyway, I ended up without a home and living in transitional housing. I never thought I would have ended up there, but I did. I had no steady income coming in, and I had to do what I had to do. I don't believe in taking advantage of people and dating for money. I kept myself up, and *literally* had to ["transition"] myself to financially survive.

I kept it together though. I didn't abuse anything. I didn't take on any bad habits like alcohol abuse or using drugs. I didn't "throw myself" around. I have been celibate since the spring of 2007, and still am. I am saving myself for marriage this time around. Saving myself for that special someone that is right for me.

Anyway, you know what transitional housing is, right? Well, if you don't, it is a place where you pay money based on your income. At the time, I briefly received General Relief (government money), $221 a month. My room rent was $60.00 a month (utilities included). There was a laundry room on the premises, and a full sized kitchen. You are assigned chores, and there is a weekly room check. In most of these places, you have to leave by 8:00am and **cannot** return before 4pm (Monday through Friday). You have to do your chores <u>seven days a week</u>. The stay in transitional housing is temporary, and you are required to become gainfully employed **as soon as possible** in order to remain there for the length of time allowed – which is usually about a year. You have regular meetings with a staff member of the organization to discuss your progress. No drugs or alcohol is allowed in transitional housing. I didn't drink or use drugs anyway. I was there because I was broke with no place to stay, and wanted to get on my feet **<u>by myself</u>**. I felt I dug this hole – I could dig my way out. Like my younger brother Perry said, "Too many people are in the park sitting on a swing waiting for someone to push them." Then I said, "Yep, you've got to pump your legs and feet to reach the height you need to get to in life." I was able to get my own apartment within a year's time. This apartment is about three blocks from Disney Hall and The Music Center and I have lived here since April of 2011. The view from my patio is the Department of Water and Power on Hope Street (the building with the golden lit top), a number of roof tops, and some palm trees. A couple of my immediate goals.....to purchase a home as soon as possible, and buy a brand new Audi.

Friend, if ever you find yourself in need of a referral for transitional housing in Los Angeles, or for temporary emergency shelter, I believe the phone number is still 2-1-1. Never be ashamed to get help for yourself – I don't care what kind of help it is. As long as you try to live ethically and morally, you will be alright. Sometimes we have to **endure**, amen.

While I was getting my skin care regimen down at a young age, I should have (at the same time) put an investment plan in place for my future.

I said that to say this: save for a rainy day because the sun may not shine for a minute, and that day may end up being months. Start saving at a young age, seriously. No one ever stressed to me how important this can be.

A good investment plan for someone around eighteen years of age or so is mutual funds. Start with about $1000 down, and then around $100 a month from that point forward. After completion of college, and landing a job with a decent income, speak to a financial advisor to find out what it takes to save and invest for a **comfortable** retirement. Discuss 401(k) plans and IRA accounts. Trust me, whatever money you need to invest - you won't even miss it! It becomes habit forming, and *this is a good habit*. At some point you will retire and you want to be prepared financially. Also, keep a savings account set aside (with available/liquid cash) for unexpected expenses or emergencies. **Try not to touch this account**.

When **stressful times** come – you want to **stay as calm as possible**. One way I do this is listening to music. I have select songs and artists I listen to. I like **Najee's** CD "Mind over Matter" – selection number six "The Journey" – that's my song. **Dave Koz's** CD "Hello Tomorrow" is awesome. On this CD selections 3, 7, and 8 are my favorites. I absolutely wear out #3 – It's Always Been You. **CeCe Winan's** CD "For Always…The Best of CeCe. On this CD "Alabaster Box," and "I Surrender All" are my favorites. When I need to gear up for power and strength, **Mariah Carey's** song

"Hero" is what I listen to. I have cried so many times to this song and gotten up and charged up again and made it. Another favorite is **R. Kelley's** "I Believe I Can Fly." These songs help me stay **focused, calm,** and **relaxed. Celine Dion's** song goes a little like this: "You were my strength when I was weak. You were my voice when I couldn't speak. You were my eyes when I couldn't see." The song simply says "Because you loved me." This song touches my heart so much and it gives me **inner strength**. *The power of the voice is amazing.*

As big as this world is, sometimes you can feel like you are here alone, and all by yourself. But you are not. There is someone that has probably experienced some of the things that you have gone through in life (maybe not all things, but some). You might be able to find someone that you can connect with on certain matters, but if you don't – you can probably "feel it" through songs. On **Eric Benét's** 2012 CD "The One", there is a selection titled, "**Lay it Down.**" Feel the song. Feel the meaning. Feel okay for a moment. There are people in this world that understand and care. Even if you don't know them personally, people can relate.

Psalm 108 1-4 says, "O God, my heart is steadfast; I will sing and give praise, even with my glory. Awake, lute and harp! I will awaken the dawn. I will praise You, O Lord, among the peoples, and I will sing praises to You among the nations. For Your mercy is great above the heavens, and Your truth reaches to the clouds."

After coming out of real estate full-time, I worked as a leasing consultant in property management for a couple of years. In one of the apartment communities I worked at in West Hollywood, there was a computer area for resident use inside of the leasing office. One evening, when it was time to close the office for the day, a resident tried to hang around longer than the hours of operation. A nice song was playing and I was singing along. I stopped singing and said, "The office is closing," and he told me he lost track of time because he was listening to me sing. He asked me if I sing from my heart, I said, "Yes, I do." He then said he could tell because my voice was so moving and sweet. I thanked him for the compliment. I used to sing in the church choir and noticed when I sang certain solos people would cry – their emotions to the songs ran so deep. You see, *music and singing can affect you* in many ways, and can have a serious impact on the body and the mind.

When I was in transitional housing, I took a job in retail for a few months, then ended up working a desk job as an administrative clerk – data entry. I did what I had to do to keep money in my pocket and pay the bills. I started paralegal school in March of 2010, and completed my studies with an associate's degree (graduating at the top of my class), in January, 2012. Obviously these jobs could not amount to what a real estate commission would be, but this was *my reality* for a moment.

Preparing for a rainy day also means keeping your résumé current. Current *meaning* having skills to qualify for positions where you can easily fit in if needed and still earn a decent income so not to struggle financially. Even if you presently have your own business, or you maintain a household, but don't work for anyone else – make sure your résumé has marketable skills. Have the skills and ability needed to work in an office environment, or on a sales team (inside sales *and* outside sales). **Volunteer** at a school or another institution. Volunteer at a church, the Goodwill, or Salvation Army. Have **at least** an intermediate skill level in frequently/commonly used software programs such as Word, Excel, Outlook, etc. There are tutorials for these programs. You can even go to You Tube for training sessions and practice tests. Make sure your telephone skills and customer service skills are sharp and professional. Know office filing systems. Be prepared for an interview, and *how to interview*. Stay on top of this because it changes more often than you think it does. And most of all, be prepared and polished for the interview – dress sharp. If you don't have the attire, check with churches and other organizations that receive donations. In this day and time, if you do not have a résumé that clearly shows you have been in the workforce recently, or volunteering your time – employers tend to look at you as someone that is out of touch and as someone they feel would not be strong enough for the position. I feel that a person should always be at least fifteen minutes early for interviews. In my opinion, if you are on time – you are late! This rule, to me, should also apply when you are **working**. Come in early. Don't sign in at your scheduled time of 8:00am – then spend five minutes in the restroom, five minutes getting coffee or tea, and five minutes chatting with coworkers. If you do this regularly – you are actually *starting* work at 8:15am not 8:00am. And yes, the boss does notice.

(For the people out there that regularly throw away last season's clothes – please donate your clothes and shoes to charity. You never know who will need your donation).

Young people don't be afraid to get your education. Stop dwelling on what you don't have. There are a number of places that give away donated laptop computers, back packs and school supplies. There are funds available to go to school. Loans and grants are available, and there are a number of companies that give scholarships for certain trades and professions. These same companies sometimes offer internships and may even hire you in the future. **Seek and you shall find.**

If you need assistance in your job search, a good employment agency is Apple One Employment Services. I have used Apple One in the past. Apple One is an excellent company and they are very good at what they do. Their website address is www.appleone.com. When you contact an employment agency, always be professional and be prepared. Have a current résumé, and do what it takes to become employed. Employment agencies can assist you with your job search, so always be professional *and* respectful with the employment agency representative.

You don't want to end up destitute. You want to be ready for the good things life has to offer. Be ready to take hold of it. You want to grab and hold on to it, and not let go. If it is meant to be yours, you shall have it. And if you had it, and desire to possess it again – you will. If you have read the Bible some, you may have read the book of Job a little bit. Go to Job chapter 28 and read from 12 through 28. Know/Knowledge – have wisdom. You know what happened in Job 42:10, right? Yes, Job received his blessings and was given twice as much as he had before. Be kind to people. Sincerely pray for others. Do not cause harm to others if you can help it. Don't cut your blessings short. You don't know what your days are going to be. You don't know the day or the hour you will leave this Earth. Be ready. Be prepared. Not just for here, but for beyond. You have no idea what is waiting for you on the other side. *Proverbs 19:8 says, "He who gets wisdom loves his own soul; He who keeps understanding will find good."*

Some people don't get to live as long as they would like, or as long as we would love to see them here.

I lost my six year old niece and her mother Labor Day weekend in 2012. My brother Perry's other two daughters, Quiara Grey and Janae Grey, survived. Quiara graduated this year with honors from Crenshaw High School in Los Angeles, and is presently attending UC Riverside. Janae is now in the 9th grade.

I lost my father to alcoholism/cirrhosis of the liver, when I was 27 years old (three months before my 28th birthday). I had to go back to Birmingham, Alabama to bury my father. He was only 51 years old – a few months shy of his 52nd birthday.

My maternal grandmother was walking home one evening from church in Birmingham, Alabama when she was beaten to death. I will never forget that day. My mother had to immediately leave. She took my baby sister Deanna with her. It was an extremely sad day. My mother had just had her seventh child. The last three of my parent's children my grandmother would never see in person because the last three, my sisters, were all born in Los Angeles, California.

My friend Cidney, the RN, said she lost a 24 year old male patient recently to alcoholism/cirrhosis of the liver. Enjoy good wine, but don't destroy your body. Diseases do not necessarily have a targeted age group.

Untimely things happen, and tragedy can strike. Nevertheless, we that remain must keep living. We are here for a purpose.

In December of 1999, I was struck by a vehicle while coming from church one afternoon. I was walking westbound when the car hit me. When I came to, and got up, I was facing southbound. I only suffered a minor contusion on my lower right leg, and a minor contusion on my head. I had no broken bones. It was a serious accident. I remember going on top of the hood of the car, then going up in the air and backward. People said the way I was hit and came down, they thought I was dead. A Los Angeles Fireman said, "It's a miracle. You don't appear to have any broken bones, and your nylons aren't even torn."

Again, we don't want to see people leave, but for those who are here, we are here for a reason. Try to know what your purpose is.

I may have been off course in the path I have taken career-wise. I had honors English in the 12th grade in high school. We had weekly assignments to read - either articles or novels, and then we had to write a report on our reading. On one assignment given, I completed the reading, but didn't feel up to writing the report. So I just threw a paper together and turned it in *last minute*. Apparently my teacher took delight in my writing and was excited to receive my work. As I watched the look on his face, his eyes were dancing with joy. Then his eyes stopped dancing. He ripped the paper up in front of my face and sternly said, "Miss Grey, this is not your best work. I will allow you to redo your assignment. Turn it in as soon as possible." Well....I didn't want to, and I didn't. I got tired of the pressure. I purposely took a fail in the class, and made up my grade in summer school. I was still able to go forward. I did not have to repeat the 12th grade. I received my original diploma weeks after the official graduation, but I was mentally tired. I was tired of the pressure advanced courses put on you and I wanted a break. As I look back, I really know what

I was doing. I didn't want to be Mensa qualified. I didn't want to answer Mensa's letter, and I was shutting the door on anyone who would try to answer for me. I did not tell my parents about the letter from Mensa. *(By the way, how do these organizations get your academic information?)* I could have graduated high school at age 15, had my mother allowed me to be skipped a couple of grades. In elementary school, I was a gifted student academically, and I was so advanced that faculty felt I should skip a grade (twice). Each time, my mother said no. I wish she would have allowed them to advance me because toward the end of high school I became burnt-out and bored, and I no longer felt stimulation in learning. You see, my father started teaching me how to spell and know the meaning of four to five syllable words when I was two years old. You never know when your children are going to have burn-out. I feel you can start with some things *too* young, and as I got older, no one taught me how to take a break, relax, calm down, and then continue. **No one did**. And this can be overwhelming. In short, I sabotaged myself for immediate development that would have enhanced my education. I also put myself in a disadvantaged position because I created limitations as far as receiving benefits from organizations that would have stemmed from acquired <u>further</u> education. This obviously affected my chances of possibly having superior career opportunities at a very young age.

I said that to say, I may have a gift to write. A gift that would well serve others. A gift that may possibly be a blessing. A gift that should not be suppressed any longer.

I write poetry occasionally. People seem to look forward to the thoughts I pen. I also know that many enjoy my conversation. I don't mind being a blessing to others. So I will share of my mind. I don't have to drive to that – it flows from me naturally. Maybe this is my purpose.

I became a member of the City of Refuge in 2008. This is Bishop Noel Jones' ministry. Noel Jones is a <u>powerful</u> pastor in the Word and with his teachings. I still consider myself a member although

I haven't been present in the congregation since last fall. I have given Bishop Jones a few inspiring and motivating writings. He also enjoys my work. Bishop Noel Jones believes I have a gift and he won't let me escape that. I remember once in church he preached a sermon about exercising your gifts. He said some firm words in that message, then he seemed to look in my direction. I looked around me, then back at him. Bishop looked at me, raised his eyebrows, then had a look on his face as if to say, "Yeah, I'm talking about you." There has been a few times that I visited other churches when he would stay "stuck" on this message. It seems as if Bishop knew where I was because the other pastors would say something like, "It's good to have such saints in the house," would look at me, then begin preaching on exercising your gifts. Another day at church, Bishop Noel Jones talked about gifts again, looked at me, then seemed to be disappointed. I felt bad. He said, "Do not leave this world and no one knows you were here. God gave you a gift, use it."

Three days after my surgery, I thought of what Bishop Noel Jones said about leaving this world, and no one knowing that you were here. I reflected on the fact that I should apply myself in this area. But the scariest part was this: what if I left this world sooner than I wanted to and had not exercised my gift? Would Bishop come to me on the other side reminding me of what I did not do, and how I did not share God's work with the world? I would not be able to bear it, because I know once you leave this world you don't know what's going to happen on the other side. And I thought, would God allow him to come over there some kind of way and keep at his message and keep drilling me? I am not taking that chance. So yeah, I started writing less than three months after surgery.

I know Noel Jones knows I am writing this book even without me personally telling him because he has access. All I can say is, Bishop, don't tell the world about this book before it is published.

I will return to the City of Refuge when I have my own private automobile. The City of Refuge is more than an hour's commute on the bus. The ride began to tire me for some reason a year or so ago and I have to guess it was because I was sick and didn't know it. Not only that, but he has a fan club. They usually sit in the first five rows of the church (the middle section). I don't think Bishop knows it though. You can see them. Just before he comes out women start touching up their hair and checking their make-up. These women act is if marvelous Marvin Gaye (how Marvin was back in the day) was about to perform. He is a preacher – not a performer. Anyway, every now and again he would look my way and smile. But he smiles at a lot of people. This didn't seem to matter to his fan club, because too many times have I had my feet stepped on or my hair pulled, *supposedly* on accident. One plus-sized woman stepped on my foot so hard and stayed there so long I thought she was going to take a nap. When I am sitting down, my hair goes over the top of the chair and hangs a little. Once a lady stood up, and when she got up from her chair, she grabbed a lot of my hair. This is my real hair, and that hurt. I asked the woman if she noticed all of the soft hair in her hand when she got up. She sharply said, "No," then dryly apologized. This kind of behavior and activity started in 2009. That's okay though. I will return, and when I do, that kind of behavior will not be tolerated. In the meantime, I will be at West Angeles Church of God in Christ just a little bit longer. No one pulls my hair or step on my feet there.

And for those of you who have negative thoughts about Bishop Noel Jones. You can have them. But again, he is human, and he is not perfect. I will always have a special place in my heart for Bishop Noel Jones. Thank you Bishop for the knowledge you impart. Your words of wisdom are most appreciated.

FOUR

IF I CAN THINK IT – I CAN DO IT. BE DRIVEN!

Today is September 2 – my birthday. **HAPPY BIRTHDAY TO ME!!!** God thank you for another one. I am truly blessed.

I have been discussing topics such as careers and professions, where you want to be in these areas, and what it takes to be qualified and achieve success in the same.

What does career success mean to you?

What career would get you the comfortable lifestyle you deserve <u>now</u>, that would pave the way to a comfortable retirement in the future?

What is your passion?

What would you enjoy and take pleasure in most?

What inspires you?

Do you have a niche for something that you want to get underway? Something monumental, lucrative, that would have a lasting positive impact in your life?

Have you started already? And if so, are you making any headway?

What would drive you to that point?

I am going to briefly mention a few people that I think have extreme drive and passion for their careers, absolutely love what they chose as a profession, and seem to let nothing impede their progress or stand in the way of their quest for happiness.

I am going to start with my cousin **Triscina Grey Ortiz**. She just called moments ago, in the middle of my writing, to wish me a happy birthday. Triscina is a radio personality with **WHUR** in Washington, D.C. She has been with **WHUR** since 1991 and absolutely loves the career she chose. My cousin meets and interviews many interesting people, and she is always thrilled with the excitement and variety of her profession. As a matter of fact, she just told me today that she received a call from the very talented Mr. Stevie Wonder on August 22. This *fine gentleman* called Triscina to wish her a happy birthday. That was such a thoughtful and caring thing to do. My cousin met Stevie Wonder early in her career in the mid-1980s. Triscina is married to the *amazing* Mr. William Ortiz. They have a son and a daughter (both in college). Triscina is the godmother of my son. You can *feel* Triscina's **passion** when she's on the air doing her thing at **WHUR**.

My cousin, **Mr. Michael Williams** of Comedy Act Theater, has been in the comedy business for decades. Michael has had comedy clubs in Chicago, Atlanta, and Los Angeles. Amazing talent has come through his clubs – some of which you have seen in movies and on television. Chris Tucker and D.L. Hughley are just a couple of top performers that appeared in Michael's clubs. Mr. Williams is always excited about his business. His joy is bringing entertainment to people, and he loves watching the audience have a good time. But one day Michael had to bring the business to a screeching halt. He was struck with cancer and the cancer had spread through his body. My cousin focused on getting well and made a lot of changes in his diet. Michael has been cancer free for well over ten years. He is currently in the process of putting together a number of shows, and even opening new comedy clubs in the very near future. Michael's passion is about being a success and never giving up. **Michael remains unstoppable**. Connect with Michael at Comedy Act Planet.com.

Mr. Jimmie Love. Jimmie is my son's barber and he has been cutting Christopher's hair since he was 9 years old. Christopher is now 28. Jimmie is the owner of Love AfHair Hair Salon in Cerritos, California, and he has several stylists in his employ. Jimmie was in the Navy for eight years before becoming an entrepreneur. He is married, and has a daughter in college. Through thick and thin and the ups and downs of the economy, Jimmy has kept a thriving business, kept his salon fully staffed, and has a long list of clients that he has provided services to for decades. Jimmie is the top man at doing hair for men and women. If you are ever in Cerritos, California stop in – the salon is near the Cerritos shopping center. The phone number to Love AfHair is (562) 809-5683.

Mr. Dulany Hill. Entrepreneur, husband, and father. Dulany has an MBA from USC and has owned his own mortgage company and real estate firm. Dulany has been in the real estate business for 30 years and in the lending business for 25 years. He specializes in investment property, and property management. Dulany has sold hundreds and hundreds of homes, and has successfully closed thousands of loans in his career. Dulany has closed many of my client's loans. Dulany Hill is a very hard working man, and is raising three young sons to be as hard working, educated, and as passionate about life, business, and helping others as he is. Dulany's desire for helping others is off the chart. Mr. Hill is also concerned about planet Earth and what is in store for our children and our future. One of his business ventures is Go US Solar. Go US Solar only sells US products, and services residential and commercial customers. You can go to goussolar.com if you desire information regarding solar for your home or business.

Mr. Hill stays motivated and always has a winning attitude. With Dulany, you get results and you get them fast. He believes in helping people reach their goals, and will do everything in his power to make it happen. Dulany is the true meaning of what a hard working entrepreneur should be. He is at the top of his game and knows how to stay there. Dulany says he is a God fearing man, and he wakes up every morning knowing who is directing him throughout the day.

Real Estate Dreams and Investments is located in Redondo Beach, California and the company services most of the southern California area. If you need a real estate agent and want results fast – call Dulany Hill.

My uncle **Walter Grey** is my father's eldest brother. Born in Birmingham, Alabama in the 1930's – he has seen many changes. His parents, Walter Grey, Sr. and Virginia, had five sons together. My uncle Walter started his career by serving in the Army. After the military, he started a career with Connecticut Transit, and within fifteen years of being employed with the company, Uncle Walter became the first black supervisor. He would retire from Connecticut Transit after 30 years of employment. Walter enjoys working with the public, he loves all people, and is a fine example of a hardworking, dedicated man. My uncle was married to my Aunt Loretta for many years. The couple has three sons and one daughter together.

Mr. Harold Lee Grey. The third son born to my paternal grandparents. This man works so hard. He retired with Connecticut Transit after 32 years of employment – then came out of retirement, and now works for the same company part-time. Before starting a career with Connecticut Transit, Uncle Harold was a chef for 13 years in Birmingham, Alabama. He joined the Masons in February, 1975, and is now a 33rd degree Mason. My uncle Harold and Aunt Charlotte have been married for over 50 years and they have two beautiful daughters together, a grandson, and a granddaughter.

Mr. Philip Whitley Lankford. Entrepreneur, Hair Stylist, and Artist. Before becoming a full-time hair stylist, Philip spent some time acting and modeling and did fairly well in both. Philip has been at Simply Raw Hair Designs in Los Angeles since 1991. Philip says, "You have to take the necessary steps to reach your goal." Philip made it clear that his purpose is to make people **look good**. When Philip was doing my hair a couple of days ago (September 4) he recalled one time when there was a power outage in the area of the salon. He said that did not stop him. Philip said he had his clients in the salon that day come to his home to complete his services. Hair that needed to be blow-dried, colored, cut, and everything else came to his home in Los Angeles - because again, his purpose is to make people look good! And by the way, if you ever want a custom painting – you have no idea. Give him a call (323) 930-2750.

Loretta Cotton is a hair stylist, custom jewelry maker, and she makes beautiful wigs. Loretta has been a professional stylist for 18 years, and she is also with Simply Raw Hair Design in Los Angeles. This woman can do twists, natural looks, and all kinds of amazing hairdos. Loretta has so much energy. You should see her "zip" around the salon. Don't even try to keep up with her. If you are looking for something very unique, Loretta can be reached at (310) 733-7308 or, leave her a message at (323) 930-2750.

A lot you have had heard of the rapper and businessman **Jay Z** aka Shawn Carter. This man is driven. Jay Z has so much energy he makes my head spin. This man is so multi-talented – what can't he do? From what I can see, Jay Z definitely can do anything he sets his mind to, and he appears not to hesitate to get it done. He has come a long way. The man's life story is very interesting. If he can do it – you can. Don't ever say you don't have possibilities or opportunity. The realization of your dream is out there. And to be honest, in this day and time, you don't have to look too hard to find it. Jay Z has the energy of a fully charged 20 year-old, and I don't think he is going to stop too soon. I remember when my son was in high school and Jay-Z announced he was putting out his last album, the Black album I believe it was. I love rap music (the radio versions) and my son knows this. I was driving my son to school one morning and Christopher said, "Mom, Jay-Z said he is making his last album. It's the last one he'll make." My son looked in my eyes as if he was telling on Jay-Z and he wanted me to do something about it. I looked at my son and said, "Christopher, that won't be Jay-Z's last album. He looks like someone who can't stop. And he won't stop." That was in the early 2000's. Where are we now? Exactly....2014. Like I said – he can't stop. *Jay Z is driven with passion and power.*

Sean Combs...aka P. Diddy....aka Puff Daddy. Smooth as the finest silk and always will be. Mr. Combs knows how to bring his thoughts into reality, and he shares his success with others. He has helped countless people with their careers. Diddy can be the background voice on my CD *anytime*. What he did in the nineties with the Notorious B.I.G. was so cool it was always hot. Puff Daddy blew my mind with his voice in the background. All I would like to hear him say on my CD is, "Mic check, yeah, yeah." His Sean Jean wear is what's up. I would buy that gear for my son when he was in high school. This is a quality line of clothing that is well worth the money. *Sean Combs himself is a story of success.*

Mr. Jamie Foxx. A man that is in a league by himself. I am truly at a loss for words on this one. He amazes me. Every time you think you have Mr. Foxx figured out, he goes and does something new, refreshing, and interesting. Jamie Foxx will forever be one of my all-time favorite actors. The article on Mr. Foxx in the May, 2014 issue of Success Magazine speaks for itself. This article had me in actual tears a few times. I could not read it in one sitting. I didn't know the man came from so far, and could get so deep. Mad props to you Jamie. I will always have respect and love for you. *Jamie, you are truly one of the best.*

In every one mentioned above, you can see that <u>hard work</u>, <u>dedication</u>, and <u>focus</u> pays off. It takes **discipline to accomplish** and realize any goal. From relationships to careers; discipline, hard work, and patience are all factors in this kind of success.

Some of us have "given" talent that is in us from a very young age, and we grow from this and develop this gift - this talent - and ability as we age and mature. For others, it could be something that is learned and a passion grows from that knowledge.

For me, I believe it is something – an assignment, if you will – that God wants me to complete for his people in the era we are in. Words He wants me to convey that would have a profound impact on society.

I was struck by a car in December of 1999. Months before the accident took place, I had a dream of death. In my dream I was walking in a cemetery to a grave site. I looked down and saw myself in a coffin. I remember waking up in a sweat, and all I kept saying to God was, "No," that I was not going yet because I have a son to raise." At the time, my son was 13 years old. I kept saying, "No God, no, I am not leaving." I kept saying, "We are going to have to work something out because I cannot go right now." I kept reading Psalm 23 every single day. I kept reading this until I got an answer. I received an answer, and that answer was that my life would be spared because I sincerely care about and love God's people. I was hit by that car, but I survived. Sure, I would pray for people – always. I was there when someone needed me. But deep down inside I knew I had a "bigger" work to do for God (a large assignment that I feel He placed on my life). And in my heart I knew it, but I never did any more than a one-on-one prayer or scripture reading with people. Never. Aside from group discussions in classes I would take at church, I never did anything more.

When I was at Re/Max (I believe the year was around 2005), we had a motivational guest speaker. This gentleman was in full speed with his seminar then, smack in the middle of his speech, he turned to me and said, "You. You are supposed to have your own company and be very successful. There is something you are **not** doing." I sat there thinking - out of about 60 agents he turns to me and says that in front of everyone. Again, deep down inside I knew what he was talking about and it wasn't real estate.

Landmark Forum called me in early 2007 and asked if I would be interested in being a room monitor – kind of like someone on the side to motivate and keep participants encouraged when they needed an extra boost. My answer to that was, "Who is going to be there for me? And until I get it figured out and become successful at what I have set out to do, I cannot see myself going "all-in" helping someone else and having regular conversations with people that are struggling with *their thoughts*. Real estate is not doing well right now and *my* deals are falling apart!" I was frustrated because the rules of the business were changing left and right. If a buyer was qualified, the rules changed to make them unqualified. Seller's tried to get a little greedier by raising prices last minute *while in escrow* – buyers were pulling out, and so on and so forth. I had never experienced so many fall-outs in my career – my fall-out ratio was **very minimal**. I lost about $45,000 in less than a three month period. **Landmark Forum is great**, and they have a lot to offer, but at the time, I was irritated and could not think of anything else but what was going on in *my* practice. I *became selfish* at that point, and could not see left or right - only straight, and that was my business. For the first time I saw something that I put a lot of energy into _literally_ fall apart before my eyes. I did not want to hear about anything else. No one was there to give me support – not in a conversation – not even as far as having a moment of peace. **It was rough**. I calmed myself with silence, thought, and meditation. Things became very clear. ***You realize quite a bit in your calmest moments***. This is when I came to the conclusion that the high school teacher I was dating was not for me. He was a selfish, self-centered person, and a little of that probably rubbed off on me. The only difference was, in his selfishness he didn't care about anyone else's happiness. I care about the happiness and content of others. It is my joy to bring happiness. I don't like misery. I was selfish about not putting energy into finding out "how to" position myself for God. At that time it didn't just flow to me like it is right now, and I really didn't know what I should do in the church, or what I should focus on specifically when it came to being there for God and His people. I should have taken the time to personally consult with a church member to see how I should exercise my gift. Then, there was a part of me that felt like "what if I mess up?" What if something happened in someone's life because of something I did or said, and I mess up? That cold stopped me in my tracks. I think it was the feeling of being responsible if something devastating happened and it lead back to me.

Well, I realize this: I do have something to share. I believe that my experiences and knowledge of life can help others that have been where I have been, or maybe prevent someone from going where I have gone. Someone could probably avoid stepping in pitfalls that I fell in. Someone could possibly avoid some pain or unhappiness that I experienced. And if they have experienced those moments of dissatisfaction – then maybe I can share something to help them get through it or understand it better. This does not take perfection or feeling wrong. This is only showing love, care, and concern. I don't have to fear doing this, I don't have to run away from it, and I have no reason to not do what God will have me do for Him. Here, I am simply giving of myself - giving happiness, peace, and knowledge. And that is nothing to be scared of.

I have been in church all of my life. My paternal grandfather was a Baptist preacher in Birmingham, Alabama. **Reverend Walter George Grey, Sr**. preached for over 30 years at Mount Olive Baptist Church in Birmingham, Alabama. He came a long way, and he worked hard in his lifetime. Not only did my grandfather pastor a church, but he worked in the coal mine, and he was also a substitute high school teacher. Reverend Grey was an educated man, loving husband, and a good father.

I am comfortable in sharing knowledge of the Bible and praying with *and* for others. So maybe writing is my talent. I believe the path in life has been given to us before we even got here. Maybe

Bishop Noel Jones saw this in me. Maybe he didn't want me to struggle with this gift or run away from it. Maybe, as an ordained person, he saw on me something deeper than what I saw for myself that God intended for my life. Some people truly have a divine gift and can see what you can't. There are people that want the best for you and don't want to see you suffer. You can have a connection with someone whether you are involved with them deeply/personally, or not. The connection somehow can be there. I think Bishop Noel Jones knew the consequences I would face by being disobedient to God. I know he cares. Thank you Noel Jones. I should have taken heed much sooner than now. Thank you for all of your prayers and for being there.

In *Romans 10:21* God says, *"All day long I have stretched out My hands to a disobedient and contrary people."*

I would like to come from *Psalm 25: 16-18. "Turn yourself to me, and have mercy on me, for I am desolate and afflicted. The troubles of my heart have enlarged; bring me out of my distresses! Look on my affliction and my pain, and forgive all my sins."*

Psalm 5:1-2, "Give ear to my words, O Lord, consider my meditation. Give heed to the voice of my cry."

I pray Lord, please forgive me for my sins and disobedience.

FIVE

KNOW YOUR WORTH

What's up Family! Where all my ALPHA people!!! If you are operating in the alpha state say, "Oh, yeah!"

You know, this past weekend I've been listening to the "Legend" album of Bob Marley and the Wailers. I have been really cooling out with this CD after a day of writing. <u>The entire album is extremely hot</u>, but my favorite songs are Buffalo Soldier, Redemption Song, and my all-time favorite – Punky Reggae Party. Bob Marley and the Wailer's lyrics are so deep, yet so easy to understand. I have been very much in touch with what Mr. Marley is saying even when I was as young as thirteen and fourteen years of age. Come to think of it, I would read Psalms and Proverbs nightly from ages twelve through fourteen. Anyway, I am going to continue listening to Bob Marley every night before I go to sleep until I complete the writing of this book. If you haven't already, you should check this album out – it is very interesting.

Okay…….. Did you write your goals down? Do you know what you want to accomplish within a year's time? Is it to build more success in an occupation or a company you already have, or do you want to start something new? Have you completed your short-term to long-term goals - your three month goals all the way to twelve months? I hope so.

Well, if you are starting off and don't have anything in mind, but want to have your own business, I have a few ideas for you. Some of these companies have been around for a while and are already very successful. All you have to do is jump on board. A small investment may be needed - but it is worth it. Here they are:

Avon

Mary Kay

Primerica

Amway

All great companies, and **many** people *already* use these services and products.

You can also think about selling your own goods at fairs and marketplaces. I don't know what your niche is. Maybe you can sew and are good at making clothes. Maybe you knit, or crochet. You might be good at silk screening with T-Shirts and other garments. You might be good at customizing hats, or doing art work on backpacks. You may be excellent at making jewelry, or handbags and purses. You may be good at painting portraits. Your niche might be baking pastries (custom cakes), cooking and catering events. Your creativity may be writing and typing. You may enjoy preparing résumés or typing business plans for others. No matter what your talent is, there is a place for it if you are interested in making money. Check to see if you need a business license first before operating a company or marketing your services. There may be some non-profit organizations around that can help with business license fees if you need financial assistance, or help you with writing a business plan for the type of loan that best suits your business venture.

If you desire to start a business, you probably already know the importance of good credit. So make sure your personal credit is worthy before trying to get a loan. Some institutions may want to see how strong you are individually – financially - before extending themselves to you when it comes to money, and even if you don't plan on personally guaranteeing any loans connected to your business, they just might want to see how you have carried yourself in dealing with others, payment-wise, in the past. Try to always operate your bank accounts in the "black" as much as possible. If you are not financially well off at this moment, it is better to have a small amount of money in the bank and keep your balances flowing positive than to have overdraft occurrences here, there, and everywhere. Look into what the government may have to offer when it comes to start-up capital for small businesses. You never know what flexibility you will have there.

Check your credit at least a couple of times a year to make sure what is there *is supposed to be there*. If you have to pay for this type of service – do it – it is worth it to know. Too many times have people applied for loans and received news of lines of credit that did not belong to them. I once had a prospect come in to discuss buying a home as a *first-time* buyer. After our initial consultation, I had his credit reports checked and found out he was *already* purchasing a home. This was all "news" to him. He didn't know anything about it. So you know every player in the game that was played on him was crooked.

Always be very careful when it comes to your personal information and check it regularly.

After having surgery, I contacted the social security administration to apply for benefits. I didn't want to work for at least a year after having surgery, so I applied. During the application process I was informed I had a cleaning company and I earned a little over $42,000 in 2012. I don't have a cleaning company. When I contacted the Internal Revenue Service after having surgery to let them know my taxes would be filed late because of the operation, they told me I had to make sure I filed taxes for 2013 or they would file for me. I said, "Is it that serious to be a few months late filing when you received unemployment benefits all but six weeks in the previous year?" The gentleman on the telephone told me that I have a cleaning company and I earned a little over $453,000 in 2013. I don't have a cleaning company. I broke down and cried. Here I am newly operated on for stomach cancer, out of work presently, and didn't know if I had to undergo chemotherapy or radiation to help heal my body. I wasn't crying because someone committed identity theft with my social security number, I was upset because they earned more money with my social security number in one year than I have ever earned in one year with it!!! I guess whoever they are will probably earn about a million dollars this year with my social security number if they don't get caught. I immediately filed an affidavit of identity theft, and submitted a picture ID along with a copy of my birth certificate. Apparently these people can use your information to work in this country, and can even operate a business in your name without question, but when it comes to paying the taxes on the earned income – that's all you. Had I not taken ill, I probably would not have known about this until the FBI or somebody came knocking on my door to notify me. Aside from a couple of blemishes on my credit report from a lack of money a few years ago, my background is squeaky clean. Evidently these thieves check backgrounds before they steal your information – wherever the hell they're getting the information from. So keep current with what is under your name.

One of the best ways to start the realization of any goal is visualization – actually seeing yourself having what you want. **Visualization, focus, action, and application of the knowledge** that relates to what you need to do, and **discipline** is the recipe for success. A good book to read is Brian Tracy's "No Excuses." This is a book about self-discipline and it is a winner. **You should start reading this book now**.

Every morning when you wake up, visualize yourself being the person you need to be to achieve your goals. See yourself in action. See yourself happy and walking in confidence and power. Visualize yourself meeting with the people you need to connect with to have your plans come to fruition. **See yourself making [large deposits] to your bank account [regularly].** See yourself living in the home you want to live in, driving the <u>car</u> you would like to drive, owning the suit of clothes you would like to wear, and being in the kind of personal relationship with "that special someone" you would like to be involved with. *Use your mind.* Remember the old saying, "A mind is a terrible thing to waste." It has been said that we rarely use the <u>full capacity</u> of our brain to begin with – so whatever part of your brain you are using – use it positively and to <u>maximum ability</u> to achieve the results you need to have a more comfortable life. **Remember: whatever you deposit in your mind – that is what you will withdraw and what [you will] have**. There is no doubt about this. So practice making *positive deposits* to your mind (your thoughts) daily. If you keep feeding your brain negative – nothing good will be there. Think of it this way: if you constantly go to the kitchen cabinet or the refrigerator taking out food – and never put anything back – eventually you gonna run out of food. You're going to be hungry. Basically, you are gonna starve! **Keep feeding your mind positive thoughts daily.**

If you are already in your desired occupation – then make sure you continue to take the necessary steps to stay there. Come to work on time (15 minutes early) – be on time to meetings, take good notes, and most importantly, save your notes for reference and write down <u>who</u> <u>said</u> <u>what</u> in meetings. (I know you knew that). If you have information to share with the team to make the "company" more successful as a whole – then share it! Don't be stingy with your knowledge thinking it is about you all of the time, because if you are not about the company staying on top as a whole (as mentioned earlier) - the company you work for may end up on the bottom. Salary increases may begin to come in minimal amounts (if at all) - the company is now barely staying afloat, and it just might go under. So all the information you kept under wraps trying to make your personal production look good will now be able to shine on your résumé when you're looking for another job. Strength comes in numbers, and contrary to what you may believe, sometimes you cannot do everything all at once *yourself.*

Divide the pie of information that you are hoarding so everyone can take a piece and work on it. This is for the betterment of the company and it will also show you as a true team member - and maybe even a leader. That executive vice president position or leadership role you were looking for is right around the corner. Always be a positive player within your group at work. Keep in mind, when looking for a job, many companies will ask you for personal <u>and</u> professional references. Be able to provide at least five <u>verifiable</u> of each.

If you are the boss, don't be a "barking boss" yelling and screaming at people all the time. How would you like it if your clients or customers constantly yelled and screamed at you? Let me answer that one for you. **YOU WOULDN'T LIKE IT!** Yelling is disrespectful, discourteous, and inconsiderate. Yelling is a <u>sorry</u> play of power, and anyone in their right mind should not tolerate it. If you have customers that take pleasure in yelling and screaming at you and your staff, then have the courage to advise them to take their business elsewhere. I don't care how much money these people are bringing in. Apparently, these type of clients think you are desperate enough to take the crap they're slinging around because you **keep** taking it. Even if it makes a big dent in the flow of cash your company receives – dismiss this client. Get a business loan to carry on until you are able to secure new clients. **Be able [to get] the loan you need to carry on** – don't put your business at jeopardy in the process. But at the same time, don't let someone walk all over you. If you got that bully of a client – you can get better clients and customers. You have to ask yourself this one question: "Would this person or company treat my competition this way – a competitor whose profits are greater than mine?" Of course they wouldn't, because people who are going places do not have time for B.S. (and I am not talking about a bachelor's of science degree). I don't care how "large" they are – arrogant and rude client's <u>suck up</u> your time and energy. People of this nature obviously feel they can disrespect you and probably think you are someone who doesn't deem yourself worthy of respect. No matter their name, level of prestige, or title – *kick them to the curb*! How many referrals do you think you are going to get from someone like that? Think about it. If you do get referrals – the referred party will probably treat you the same way because they *think they can.* It is better to have ten smaller accounts from people you feel comfortable with and have the pleasure of working with, than to have one large pain as a client. If you don't look out for yourself and respect yourself why should anyone else feel that way for you? Especially in business. I repeat, especially in business. Why should they? You have to give them a reason to respect you and to honor your word as a professional <u>from the beginning</u> of the relationship – and this takes confidence. Because if you don't – and they do business with you – in the back of their mind your name is "doormat." There it is. And in case you haven't figured it out, these last few paragraphs can be applied to your personal life as well, if you are in that position.

BOSSES: You are not at war with your staff. The **mutual goal** should be to realize the same outcome for the company - and this is **customer satisfaction and profit** – in that order. Communication should always be pleasant and effective among people. Yelling and screaming will probably run your blood pressure up and everybody else's too. And some employers have the nerve to complain about how they're constantly paying for employees to be out on stress leave. Don't drill and bang employees up mentally. Stress leave can be as simple as an employee calling out sick for two consecutive days here and there because they don't want to hear **your mouth** for a couple of days. They have to gear up mentally just to come into work to **tolerate being around [you]**. They may like their job – but not like the boss. Think about it. This kind of behavior from bosses can have a way of bringing down morale in the workplace, and people tend not to care about the company *or* the business of the company as much. So instead of you barely breaking even every year – you could realize much greater profits if you treated your staff better. Much of the reason you are just "breaking even" in your business is because your employees are performing at a mediocre level – a level that is just enough to keep your doors open and their paychecks coming. Your employees **have the**

ability to do more. You didn't dub them "mediocre" when you hired them. If that was the case, they wouldn't be there. And you weren't a "barking" person when they said "I do" and got on board with the business. So take time out to **straighten this out** before everybody loses. Don't destroy what was built. This refers to the profitability and existence of the business all the way to keeping professional relationships intact, and keeping staff on board that has the capability of being high performers.

SALES PEOPLE: You know the saying: "Every day you are not personally communicating with clients and new prospects is another day you are putting yourself closer to being out of business and without a job."

Where is your ALPHA state? If you feel tired, and busted, in need of being refreshed and revamped you better think of something real fast player or you are going to be out of the game with a quickness! It truly is as simple as that. As the saying goes: "If you don't know – you better ask somebody!" Get current and brought up to speed!

You need to get your energy level up and put your "creative hat" on **for real**. You see how we rollin' in the 21st century and being able to be a strong competitor is key – in anything. If you are a weak link in the group, there is a possibility you could get cut. Dismissed with a quickness. There are no two ways about this whether you work for yourself or for someone else – there is no gray area in this subject. If you don't know what it takes to bring in business in this day and time, or you don't know how to exactly go about it – find out real fast. (We have too many resources in the 21st century for you not to know). You don't have a personal computer you say, or you don't have internet access at home? So you feel it is not as easy for you to research information as the next person? Can you say *library*? The membership to the public library is free!

Know that it does not matter what your business is – you have to be able to effectively communicate what you are about. Communication can be face-to-face, telephone, internet, advertising in local newspapers, flyers, penny saver magazines – like that. I have noticed over the last five years that a lot of individuals and companies don't seem to advertise in penny saver magazines and local newspapers. The penny saver comes to residential mailboxes faithfully **every week**, and local **free newspapers** are **everywhere**. These forms of advertising are not that expensive to place ads in, and people read them *all of the time*. Here, people don't have to pay to pick up what you have to say. You can place ads in these sources by the week, month, or year, and it is well worth the money spent. In real estate, if I placed a monthly ad on a listing and received interested buyers (usually very easily) and sold a property within 30 days – don't you think what I paid for the ad would be worth every cent? Sure it would. It is all about how you word your advertisement. **ADVERTISE TO SELL!!!**

It doesn't matter what your product is, [sales is one of the highest paid professions] and always has been.

You don't like being told no, or you fear objections? Get over it now!!!

Even if they outright tell you "no," keep giving reasons why they should invest in or buy **your** product (whatever it is you are marketing). Express what the benefits are and why **NOW** is a good time to buy. Whatever you are selling, be prepared and have the answers to the most common objections you could receive. Remember: the customer is not necessarily saying no – they just need you to give them more reasons (underline information) why they should say yes, and buy/work with you and your company. Keep in mind that you are not the only one doing what you do in your profession. You have to know your product inside and out, be confident, and be able to sell it well. Knowledge and confidence is key in sales and if you are not strong in these areas – the spotlight will seem to shine on you at *that very moment* (as if you are on stage by yourself and messing up royally) and I promise you that you will not get the business. *Make sure your presentation* *is smooth and on point. Role play with someone in your industry, and continue to role play, until your presentation is as effective as it possibly can be.*

Be confident in your product. When I was in real estate full-time, and I called on a prospect to get a listing, and the seller had multiple agents to consider hiring to list their home – I always asked to be interviewed last. I was on top of my game. I made sure I had detailed information about the property I planned to list, and, of course, I knew the comps, stats, and as much as I could about every home for sell in the immediate area of my prospective client's home. I got the listing every single time.

I worked my listings hard. I passed out flyers in the immediate area of the listing notifying residents that an open house would take place soon, I advertised the home in the penny saver, all internet real estate sources including, of course, the multiple listing service, a for sale sign was up, and I cold called around the area of the listing – like that. I worked the property hard. I got new buyers that wanted to buy in other areas, and I even double-ended some listings. I got quite a bit of repeat and referral business – which is the name of the game because you don't have to continuously work as hard. We all know the beauty of passing out flyers around the listing. Many people have relatives and coworkers that want to buy in their area. They take their friend or family member the flyer, and boom...a property is sold. If you are in real estate, we all know the beauty of the "**<u>SOLD</u>**" sign on the property too. More interested sellers/more referrals!!!

Never take on impossible business. Never take business that will not sell well or within a reasonable amount of time. Your effort will be a complete waste. I had a prospect once that wanted to sell his home above market rate and he also wanted to discount my commission. What do you think I did? Right. I did not take the listing. I did not take the listing because he was adamant about his demands. I would not even market the listing for 30 days. Why? 1) Because advertisement costs me money. 2) The listing would become stale on the market. 3) I would be helping everyone else within the area of the listing sell *their* home faster, and 4) I **am** worth what I ask for. The prospect said, "But you sell lots of homes in this area, why can't you sell this one for what I want?" I told him it would not be a reasonable contract and that he was only helping the competition – which are his neighbors - sell their property *faster*. **KNOW YOUR WORTH**!

Also, sales people, if you are working with prospects that are "straddling the fence" and seem to have every reason in the world why they can't make a buying decision now, **stop wasting your time**. Days with these people, soon become weeks – which can become months. You have to ask yourself one question: "If I had 10 solid pieces of business in place **at this very moment** that I needed to work in order to close the deals and get paid commission and/or bonuses within 30 days, and I also had 10 very **motivated hot** prospects that needed my time to sell them what they wanted **now**, would I still be working with this **cold** prospect? Of course you wouldn't! So why do you keep calling them? You have to come from this belief **every day** to not waste your time on a regular basis. Stop pretending like you are busy when you know you are not doing anything worthwhile with these people that would lead to a paycheck!

Always know what your weekly and monthly goals should be and always make your numbers. Even if you have solid business in place, you still have to prospect every single working day as if that business is not there because anything can happen. If your deals close – GREAT! Constant prospecting will put [more money] on the books. If you are in sales, it is a must that you have a designated block of time for hard prospecting **daily**. Block out the amount of time you need to prospect in order to meet your weekly goals and let absolutely nothing take you off course. Stay motivated, and have a *winning attitude* when you prospect (*remember to smile*). Mentally come from "zero" every day as if you have no sales on the books. Keep that [**hunger**] in your system and I guarantee you will be a sales success. Every morning tell yourself, "I will have an **absolutely amazing day**." **YOU ARE A WINNER. YOU ARE A SUCCESS.**

MOTIVATIONAL SPEAKERS:

I am going to ask you three questions.

Do you believe motivational speakers are worth what they ask for?

Can you see yourself paying anywhere from $100 to $5,000 to hear someone speak?

Would you pay to listen to someone who could help boost your sales performance or the profitability of your business and almost instantly increase your income to numbers you never thought you could get to if you applied their techniques?

The answer to all of the above questions should be an emphatic yes!

If you have ever been to one of these events or seminars and were paying attention, listening closely, and taking key notes - then left and *actually exercised* what you learned and seriously applied yourself **immediately**, you would have made the money back you spent on the program over and over and over again. I have never been to a seminar, listened to a motivational speaker, applied myself, and not made back the money I spent and then some. And that is the truth. **If you take away only one new piece of knowledge from these seminars and immediately apply yourself with this ability – you would have well spent your time and money.**

This is true because **YOU** are exercising **YOUR** belief system, **YOU** now have a strong level of confidence and the trust and faith **YOU** need within **YOURSELF** to achieve **YOUR** goals with the knowledge **YOU** have gained from the seminar or program. The speaker has heightened **YOUR** sense of awareness, and more than likely woke up feelings inside of **YOU** about actual ability **YOU** have within **YOURSELF** to be the best **YOU** that **YOU** probably forgot **YOU** could be. **YOU** have been *stimulated* so much in the seminar that **YOU** have such an electric charge that if **YOU** were an automobile **YOU** wouldn't need gasoline because **YOU** are already *sizzling with energy!* **YOU** are ready to go...... move, get out of **MY** way --- **I AM READY TO DO THIS, AND I AM GOING TO HAVE AN ABSOLUTELY AMAZING DAY!!!**

I bet this one paragraph got you fired up already. Where my money? ☺

See, it all goes back to applying what you have heard and exercising faith and belief.

Friends, this is why when you are in church and the pastor has a vision and tells you to exercise faith and reach up and grab what God has for you – he is wanting you to feel the presence, feel the reality of having what is yours and claiming it. Believe this and own it. Cement your belief by planting a seed of faith. When you go to the altar and plant your seed of faith – you have to own it – mentally dress yourself with it. Continuously walk in power with this belief and do not let it go. From the time you leave the church premises until what God has for you comes – continue to dress yourself with your belief, and it shall be yours. **Belief is your new wardrobe.**

This is when you hear the testimonies of what God has done for people. What you don't understand is – it was already done. It was here waiting for you before you got here. It is not a secret. When He knew He would have you as His child – you were already blessed with your gifts and the possessions God has for you. But sometimes you have to take action, amen. This is why God says, "**seek and you shall find**."

You have to know that it was already there – it was already there family. You have to walk in positivity and faith. **BELIEVE IN YOURSELF. BELIEVE IN YOURSELF. BELIEVE IN YOURSELF.** Everything else is confirmation. It is just confirmation. But if you need the extra encouragement, there is nothing wrong with that. Always invest in yourself.

Remember: with a tight closed fist – nothing goes out – nothing comes in. You cannot receive your blessings with a tightly closed fist. Sow your seed brother. Sow your seed sister. <u>Believe in *you* and don't sell yourself short</u>. You are so precious and you deserve **the best**. So *reach up and grab* your blessings. See yourself having what God has **intended for you and only you**. God has a custom plan for everyone – no two are the same – not physically, <u>nor mentally</u>. Plant your seed and believe.

KNOW THIS: YOU MUST STAY POSITIVE TO REALIZE AND RECEIVE GREAT THINGS. POSITIVE AND GOOD <u>CANNOT</u> DWELL AND <u>REMAIN</u> WHERE NEGATIVE AND HATE LIVES.

SIX

A SWIFT KICK IN THE BUTT

Here it comes. It's about to get real.

I'm sitting here trying to figure out a way to get this chapter started because I don't know if you can take it.

You see, when I said earlier that one of my fears in doing God's work is that I was afraid that I would mess up. Truth is, I was afraid to mess <u>you up</u>. Some people are not strong enough to be rebuilt. They can't handle it. I am a lucid person. That is me. Sometimes I am outspoken and I have been told this in business – but people seem to like this side of me and they appreciate it. Candor is not always a bad thing. I am honest, and all I ever want is the best for you, and to see the good in you show. I want to *enliven* you to be who you should be. You have obstacles stopping you and you may not know what they are. You may not know why you haven't been as successful as you would like or why **YOU** haven't received **YOUR** blessings yet. I am going to mention a few *possibilities* as to why.

The mind, like the body, is very strong, but it can be weak and fragile at times. People *sometimes* cannot control their thoughts or emotions when they encounter particular problems or become involved in unpleasant situations. These experiences can create difficulty in maintaining normalcy in areas of everyday living. In these cases, some individuals may need psyche meds or need to talk to a professional conversationalist (this is my term for psychologist or a psychiatrist). As far as I am concerned, there is nothing wrong if you need a professional conversationalist or have to **temporarily** use psyche meds (if meds are *absolutely necessary*). If this is what it takes for you to be able to cope, and to not cause harm to yourself or others - then do what you have to do. The profession of psychology and psychiatry exists for a reason. Don't sit back and ball up in a knot, become a recluse, or on the other side – a violent person because your reality may be a bit overwhelming for a moment. Do not get to a point where you want to take your life or someone else's life because your thoughts go wild. Get help if you need it.

Sometimes, to go forward in life, we have to breakdown what we have in our past, or learn how to better assess things. Like an automobile, the body may be good, the tires may be okay, but you may have to make some changes and/or adjustments under the hood. The mechanic may have to take out some wires or plugs. You may need a new radiator or you may need to have your engine rebuilt. You may even need a *completely* new engine.

Before you have surgery on your body, the physician has to make sure your body will be able to handle the operation. You need to be strong enough to handle the operation!

Are you strong enough? Keep your walk with God and have strength.

We have issues we have to address if we want to *walk* in *empowerment* and in *peace*. We have to respect others, and treat people right. Treat people with the fairness and respect that you expect to have come your way. Life is not one-sided and you don't live in this world by yourself. How you perceive things is not always the way it is. You cannot always make things *mean* what you what them to *mean* (giving matters your own *interpretation/*

translation), and you cannot always control the behavior of others. People <u>are</u> who they are, and they have a given right to express themselves and be who they want to be in life as long as their expression and how they interact with others does not cause harm. Would you agree to this?

There are a few topics I would like to address. Situations, thoughts, and actions that I feel people should consider when it comes to society because of the suffocation and hindrance it creates. These are my opinions only. I believe that as a people, we should acknowledge what I am about to say because it would make life better in many areas. I am not trying to control anyone's thoughts or judge anyone. You don't see me walking around wearing a robe and hitting a gavel on a desk after I have my say. I am merely commenting on a few subjects.

First, I want to talk about **time management** and the success of your career.

You cannot let anything interfere in your workday that does not relate to work or have a direct correlation to what will bring you success in realizing your goals. That means communicating with people that have "***drama***" in their lives. Everything they are crying about is ***urgent*** and ***serious*** in nature *to them*. These people are so melodramatic they could win an Oscar for their performance. "I think my husband is leaving me, or my kid is acting up again - what should I do? My rent is due tomorrow and I don't have the money, I am so upset. Little Johnny has a game tomorrow and I don't have enough money for gas to travel that far. My neighbors are loud again, should I call the police? I have a toothache, should I go to the dentist? Girl, I just banged my foot, I wonder if it's broken – should I go to the doctor?" Stuff like this happens to people all of the time, and people who are self-employed and make their own schedule get double doses of it. You leave work and rush over to console someone. You take your hard earned money to treat them to lunch to discuss *their* problems. Then... you go over after work to join them for the pity-party they've invited you to. Stop it! You are non-productive when you engage in this kind of activity. And if you decide to join them after work, don't harbor negative feelings inside that would impede on your productivity the next day. People who do this to you on a **regular basis**, are inconsiderate and do not respect **your time**.

Don't become preoccupied with hindering or harmful/ negative thoughts. Dwelling on what happened to you, or why would he say that, or why wouldn't he/she want to see me have or be the best – so on and so forth. These are not healthy thoughts. These thoughts can cause you to have severe mental blockage, wreck your flow of creativity and performance, and leave you stuck on stupid. That was my biggest problem and I had it down to a science. I was in a fog so much because of this it was ridiculous. I knew my job well. I could sale property. I proved that time and time again. One day my broker's assistant at Re/Max was handing me a couple of checks and she said "Dorsha, how do you do that?" I said, "What?" She said how do you end up in a deficit – nothing on the books, then out of nowhere have multiple sales on the books, catch up, and end up with an increase?" I told her I prospect hard *out of nowhere* – make it happen – then handle my business." What I really wanted to tell her was that I shifted gears from "stuck on stupid" then put the gear in full-speed to <u>progress</u> and <u>forward</u>. It wasn't that I couldn't continuously sell – I just didn't. I was so good at one point that a number of new agents would come to me for coaching. It had even gotten to where one of the top producers in the office told the broker how new agents coming to me for advice should be giving me some kind of bonus on their closed transactions. I declined. I was just happy to help.

You have to **<u>ditch mental stumbling blocks</u>** as soon as you notice them. If you don't, it could destroy your success. What should have been easy, can end up being very hard and this can bring you to complete ruin. Realize that you have to stay on a positive path to have success. Travel on the plane in life where you will have <u>happiness</u>, <u>peace</u>, <u>fulfillment</u>, and <u>prosperity</u>, and if others don't like this method of transportation and what it has to offer, then let them take the lower road – because you are trying to soar, and ain't nothing down there for you. These people are just clipping <u>your wings</u>.

Don't judge people on what you see. Don't automatically think you are better than someone else. Because a person is an ex-convict, or financially less fortunate than you, or live in a neighborhood that isn't as nice as yours - doesn't make you better. Because a person has less education than you doesn't make you a better person either. Intelligence should tell you that possessions and education do not necessarily make you a better human being. People are just trying to get to where they have to go and they are not "studying" you. You probably don't have what they want anyway. So stop judging people when you sit next to them, or when you have a conversation with them. This kind of behavior is not cool.

When you see an attractive person, don't put your own label on them. This is how it goes... "Who does she think she is? Does she think she's cute?" Let me answer that for you. She **knows** who she is, and she probably is cute!

For the **insecure person** that is constantly grabbing onto their mate when someone attractive walks by, here is a clue: it takes two. If you think every attractive person walking by (usually minding *their own* business) wants your mate, then you have a problem. And I am going to tell you like this: behavior [along these lines] only leads a person to believe that what you have is not that secure and solid. And if your dude or your girl is down – that person would not have a problem getting the digits and starting a relationship with what you *thought* you had. Another thing: if you are giving your mate that much grief, you are creating constant unhappiness and drama in the relationship and that person is probably better off without you because you are insecure and you have a lot of trust issues. **Work it out!**

Church Folk:

First of all, stop running people out of the church. There are a lot of attractive single people raising children. When you see a nice looking person coming to church with their children – don't make them feel uncomfortable. That is not right. **One**, the person can't help because they were born with the looks they have. **Two**, they have a right to fellowship just like you do. **Three**, who said they want your spouse? Because they don't have a ring on their finger they want what you have? Please. *You* probably don't really want what you have. That's why you are in marriage counseling right now! (Or probably should be in counseling). This is the main reason I ended up gaining **more than 50 pounds** a couple of times in my life, and also whacked my hair off. I felt that if I weighed much more (not physically fit/not in shape) and cut my hair, that I would be more accepted. People shouldn't have to feel this way. To the attractive people that are physically fit: don't ever feel bad about how you look in order to "fit in" a group and be accepted. Always embrace who you are and love who you are. Whether you feel you have attractive features, or you feel your features are not as attractive as you would like – embrace who you are. You were created this way for a reason. **Everyone is beautiful to me**. Everyone. Everyone has something beautiful about them. We all know this. And for those of you who don't believe this – if you would stop being so superficial you would be able to see it.

Classifying by what you see:

Scenario One: You are a hardworking woman. You have your college degree, you are buying your home, you have the job you want, and your salary is "all that." You are in a grocery store shopping, a guy wearing sagging jeans, a wife-beater tee shirt and tennis shoes walks by. He looks your way – you make eye contact. You turn your nose up in the air and keep walking. He walks on. His stroll is so hard and *so cool* you'd think he owned half of the world. The next day, you are in the bank during your lunch hour, and you see the guy you saw in the grocery store. He is wearing the same style of dress…designer sagging jeans, and what appears to be a designer wife-beater tee shirt. You turn your head so not to make eye contact. He doesn't even notice you are there. This man is now at the teller's window and the teller happily addresses him by his full name. You overhear the teller saying: "Mr. ……, would you like to put the entire two million dollars in your main account, or would you like to divide the funds among your other accounts in the manner of your last deposit *a few days ago*?" All of sudden, you snap your head around toward his direction, but he still doesn't notice you. The two of you are now in the bank parking lot. You say hello to him (smiling as if you've just won the lottery), he speaks, gets in his SUV and keeps going.

What just happened Miss Pretentious (Pre-Pre)? What happened was you thought because he was dressed the way he was he couldn't measure up to *your* standards.

You see, he wasn't your type when you thought he was busted, but now that you see his money is long you think he can be trusted? Girlfriend please....you need to *seriously* quit.

Hey Pre-Pre? I bet when you were in the bank and overheard how much money he was depositing you thought he was a rapper, huh? No girl. He is a clothing designer. He has his own manufacturing company, and a number of retail stores. The clothes he is wearing - he designed, and he sells his merchandise all over the world!!! By the way, he is an ivy-league **college** educated man, and his wife is an attorney with a **successful** private practice.

What you don't understand is that success doesn't always come wrapped in expensive tailored blue suits. There are a good number of people in prison, at this very moment, for "white-collar" criminal activity.

If you keep your nose in the air all of the time Pre-Pre, you may not always be able to see what is really in front of you.

Scenario two: You are driving your Ferrari down Wilshire Boulevard in Beverly Hills. An attractive woman is in your view. She is walking down the sidewalk. You rev your engine to get her attention – she keeps walking. She is now walking past your car. You back up a little and park. She notices all of your effort. She walks toward you – says hello, tells you she admires your automobile and asks you to pop the hood. You then get out of the vehicle with *excitement*. She looks under the hood and loves what she sees. She tells you *the engine is awesome* - then thanks you for showing her your sports car. From there, she tells you to have a nice day.

What just happened Mr. "I need money to get the honeys?" I can tell you exactly what happened because that was me a number of years ago. He did not get my phone number. Two reasons: 1) I felt he was putting me in a box by thinking because he had an expensive car (indicating he might be financially well-off) that I would date him. 2) If that is all he thought of himself – then I did not want to deal with him.

I did this to this guy because this has happened to me several times and I got tired of it. So I teased him by showing interest – then I kept going. Maybe he learned a lesson.

Yo, money! Stop playing yourself. Just because a woman looks like she is about something, carries herself well and with confidence, and has a little bit of looks, doesn't mean she is shallow or a gold digger. Think better of yourself and want more for yourself. You will get what you ask for **every time** – no matter what it is, because that is the "*law of attraction*" you are *applying* to your life.

Those with issues against people that are LGBT: Yeah, I am going there. Okay, we know what the Bible says on this subject, but again, we are not here to judge. God did not give you the assignment of judging people. Yes, we can have our opinions, but in public, keep your negative thoughts to yourself. Do not approach someone who is gay and harass them. How would you like it if you were approached and harassed because you are not gay? There are laws and prisons for your actions when it comes to what your definition of "normal" is. Your words, your harm, your vandalism to property, and your violence will not be tolerated in society. This behavior toward anyone is not acceptable - no matter what their sexual preference is. No one wants to see you in jail because you want to exercise your strong point of view directly toward someone and cause harm in the process. No one wants to see you there. Why would you take away from yourself and cause destruction of who you are as a person because of how you feel? Could you hate someone that much? You could hate someone so much that you would mess up how you live presently (possibly taking away your freedom), and jeopardize how you would be able to live in the future because of this? Don't be that way. Hate is one of the strongest emotions to have, and it is also the most negative and damaging of all. **You can actually cause <u>self-destruction</u> with hate**. Hate affects your mind and the overall health of your body. Hate can destroy relationships. Hate can cause you to lose your job. Hate can make you think so unclear that you mess up your finances. **Hate destroys life.**

Don't hate.

I am not trying to tell people how to love their children, but please, please, please, do not disown your son or daughter because they didn't end up the way **you wanted** them to.

No child should have to feel like they should take their life because you took your love away. No one should end up overdosing, or killing themselves because they don't feel free to express themselves – especially around you – their family. No one should have to hide who they *truly* are. They **should not** have to hide at work, at school, or at church.

If you have a family member or friend that has told you they prefer the same sex as their mate, do not destroy your relationship with that person because of their preference. Maybe for you this would be a hard "pill to swallow," but take your medicine and move forward with them in life. Don't hurt them. Please don't make someone feel bad because you want to feel right. Do you think it would be better for you to come out of "your box" and try to be <u>understanding</u>, <u>caring</u>, and <u>loving</u>, or do you think it would be better to end up seeing them in a box, at their grave site, sooner than they should because you weren't reasonable?

Church people should know better. You read the Bible all of the time and you know it is not your position to judge. Your tacit behavior and your malevolence toward others that you feel are not like you should stop. And after everything you have done, you want to secede from the church where you **fellowship** because too many of whom you don't like now attend. You mumble to yourself about who you think is going straight to hell, and who you think is going to burst hell wide-open. I am not saying I want to be in hell when the roll is called – but it is going to be very interesting. Again, I am not judging you, but wrong is wrong, and right is right.

There are actually ignorant people who think they are going to catch something if they hug someone who is gay or shake a gay person's hand. What do you think is going to happen if you show a little kindness and affection? And don't fake it. If you don't like them - you don't have to. Everyone doesn't like you either. But don't get upset with someone because they are comfortable with who they are. It is not a crime if a person is comfortable with their being and they are able to define themselves with confidence. If gay people are okay with who you are, why can't you be okay with who they are? Stop tripping. They are probably not even thinking about you. You might not even be their type. So you can stop running. What's up?!

INTELLECTUAL PROPERTY!

What's up with people that steal people's work? A sister got wind of some *stuff* recently.

If you are reading my material before it hits the bookstores and the internet **for sale and for (my) profit**, then you have an *unauthorized* distributed copy. I have not given anyone – I repeat – anyone, permission to read and/or distribute the writing of this book prior to publication. This book will be titled "I Am Not Finished Yet," and I'm gonna tell you like this: I have a very unique style of writing. This book will not be professionally edited for certain reasons. I read the internet regularly and have noticed, here recently, certain traits of writing out there similar to my style of writing. Along with this, I have also noticed things that are taking place that directly relate to subjects I have mentioned in this book-to-be – with words I have specifically used, and I don't think this is a coincidence. *If I ever find out "firsthand" who you are – I am going to sue you. I am going to sue you so hard it is going to blow you away. I am going to come to your ass so fast for correctness.....as fast as the speed of sound in water, and as hard as sonic boom force!*

I don't care who you are – you will have it coming to you. This goes for my book "I Am Not Finished Yet", as well as my writings of "The Final Test (No One is Exempt)," and the writing "The Final Test Is A Reality." The Final Test series were both written August, 2013. So no, I am not finished yet, and don't let me find out about your shadiness because there will be consequences. I may still be learning how to use the touch screen cell phone I purchased two months ago, and I may not have the desire to learn how to text message, but I am not stupid. I know how to read, and I stay on the internet. Don't laugh. This is not a laughing matter. I am as serious as you are scandalous. This is worse than when people bootleg movies. At least the bootlegged movie is a finished product. My shit is being distributed and it's not near completion.

You haven't come to me correctly because you haven't gotten your *stuff* together yet, or is it because I don't earn enough money, or both? You know who you are! Whatever the underlying reason, you cannot just take my name and spread it all over the world connecting me to you when it is convenient for you. You and I both know I am a good woman - one of the best - and it doesn't work that way. You need to come to me *correctly*. But since this is how you presently feel, I'll tell you this: when I come up... you can catch my vapors, because I may not want you in the same space breathing the same air I breathe when I am blessed financially. I need to help myself, my family, and others, and you have the audacity to take from me? **What are you thinking?** You, or someone you hired, entered my computer without permission and took my information and shared it with people. You are hurting me and my progress, and this is a clear case of someone stifling a person's growth and not showing respect. What would make you any better than the high school teacher I dated? He may have "*voiced*" his feelings about the fact that he didn't want to see me successful and living a better lifestyle, but you stealing my property and *freely* distributing it is taking away **my ability** to earn a decent income to better myself. In a way, what you are doing is worse. Please explain to me how your actions would constitute care for someone. Given my current situation, if part of my goal wasn't to earn money while trying to help others, I would be on a street corner with a loud speaker sharing my thoughts *freely*.

Let me school you brother man. In case you didn't know, this shit is in **hard distribution**. Whoever you are "*sharing*" my knowledge and creativity with, they are freely sharing it, as well. You guys are passing my stuff around like it's a modern day underground railroad to freedom. These people are not your friends and they are not trying to be friends of mine. As the saying goes, "with friends like these, who needs **enemies**." And in case you don't know, this is how you get your *frenemies*.

Oh, she said some bad words! I told you in the beginning I am not perfect. And yeah, when I become angry sometimes I use profanity. And yes, I do know what the Bible says about this – but **you** are not my judge. I am not signing up to be a role model for your children. That's **your** job. Be glad that's all I do is use profanity occasionally when I get angry. This is something I obviously have to work on. If there weren't laws and prisons in place, a whole lot of folks would get "straight worked" when it comes to me and the shit they pull. I would first let you know who they are by wearing a glove, heavily coating the glove with white powder, and literally slapping the hell that's in them right out! On the right side of their face.... JUST BAM...slap they ass silly!! Everyone would know that you must have pissed Dorsha Grey off because you have the print of a powdered hand slap on your face. You are probably laughing, but I am very serious. Be lucky for laws and jails because this truly angers me.

This is what's up. I wrote a letter to a particular someone this summer clearly stating I had a gastrectomy in March due to stomach cancer, and that I had no income coming in at the moment. I asked that person to help me financially because of this, and also because I was in the process of writing a book and wanted to get the book out immediately. I don't even have a car. I have a perfect driving record, but I have not been able to afford another car lately. I go to the doctor for check- ups and I really shouldn't be on the bus. When I go to church – I have to take a bus and a metro train. I have a sister with five children and she is presently unemployed. I am trying to help her whenever I can because I know things can be hard financially at times. My mother is on a *fixed* income that is *low* – she is 73 years old, and I would also like to be able to help my brother's two remaining living daughters. I only receive $1402 a month from Social Security (as of August, 2014). I ask you for help - you know the situation of <u>everything</u>, and you would take from me with this knowledge? This is not cool. Don't let God have to chastise you for this. You wouldn't acknowledge me, but you would take from me? Right your wrong brother! You can send the money I asked you for to P.O. Box 14473, Long Beach, CA 90853. This is the post office box I have had since 1997 – it is in Belmont Shore about a mile or so from the Re/Max office I worked at on Pacific Coast Highway in Long Beach from 1997 until 2008. You know where it is. I am not playing. This is foul. Handle your business. You ain't never done nothin' for me, and I ask you to do something *one time* and you can't do it *knowing [everything else] you have done*. What's up with that? I have <u>never</u> slept with a man for anything when it comes to survival, and I don't deal with people of prestige to try to bite off their action. If that was the case, and if I was remotely close to being that kind of woman, my ass would not have ended up in a shelter and transitional housing. For some reason, men of wealth have always been attracted to me and they still are. It has been this way for me since my early twenties, and trust, I am still fine enough to pull that kind of action, if I really wanted to, *today*. I just don't believe in taking people for granted, and I am not going to date a person solely for their wealth – not now – **not**

ever! I like to earn my own money. Don't steal my money by jacking my project.

Anyone that intends on practicing law – I have one tip for you: Intellectual Property Law. Study it. Do it. Make your money. Make your money because so many people want fast money – want fresh ideas and new information to make money, but they don't want to take the time to think or be [original]. And lawyer-to-be, if you don't think you can become **very** rich in this area of law - in this day and time – then you would not be applying **yourself**. With all of this "*so-called*" technology regarding security for computers, scandalous ass people are still able to break into your computer system and steal your stuff. Hell, they check your email before you do! Seriously future attorneys, there are so many lazy people out there that have become so tepid about what they are doing in their walk in life, that instead of putting conscious effort into what their "*so-called*" passion is – they find it easier to take advantage of hardworking kindhearted people. Not only are these people lacking consciousness of what they should be doing….they have no conscious when it comes to how they mess over others. So when they feel it's time to increase their profits (the bottom line in **their** bank account) they wanna rob somebody else. I don't appreciate this, so yeah, I have an in-your-face attitude about it, and I have a right to feel this way.

SEVEN

SUM IT UP

Okay, I am calm now. But on the real, come on family----I know you feel me on this. Today is September 14, 2014 and I received validation of this **madness** yesterday. I will also truthfully tell you this: fifty percent of my delayed writing on these subjects was that I did not want to rattle anyone the wrong way or disturb anyone mentally when it comes to matters of life, and the other fifty percent is *I knew* this person, or someone they hired, would take my information and share it with "*buddies*." To date, I have printed *no* pages. I have verbally discussed nothing regarding the contents of this book with anyone. The only thing the few people I have told about this book knows is that this is a writing on self-development and self-improvement, and it is inspirational. That's all. So anything made public prior to distribution of the published product, is put out there in an unauthorized manner. People that steal intellectual property need a serious courtroom beat down.

My book, "I Am Not Finished Yet," will be published with AuthorHouse. If you want a copy, contact them.

TIME TO SUM IT UP!!!

Yo, Alpha, where you at?!!! Say, "I am right here, and I am going to have an **absolutely amazing day!**"

This chapter is pretty much a <u>recap</u>itulation of everything in this writing thus far, and I want to start by saying, *know* where you are going in life, and always be true to yourself in that walk. Let nothing and no one (including *yourself*) take you off this path – this course - in your greatness.

Do your best to stay focused. Try not to lose sight of where you are going. If momentary darkness comes, remember to <u>regain vision</u>. Like entering a dark room, our eyes adjust to the darkness first – then we are able to see much of what is actually there. We regain focus and go forward. You must have perception. People that don't have the use of their eyes know this well. They learn to adjust in life, and many become very successful. Some people without natural eyesight, many a times, are more focused than people that have full use of their eyes. So, we make <u>excuses</u> and find <u>reasons</u> when we don't want to perform or achieve, yes? If you are still there at this point in this book– you need to get off that track right now! And another thing, if you are there, [with no production or realization of some of your goals], then you are merely reading the book and going "through the motions" and <u>not applying yourself</u>, because at this point, you should have made some strides – you should have realized *some* <u>progress</u>.

(Take a moment to do your own personal assessment and recap from where you started to where you are now regarding the highlighted areas of this reading. Key points have definitely been emphasized in this book).

Okay.....it's September 23, 2014, 1:55PM, and I'm typing just a little bit slower because about an hour and a half ago a taxi driver smashed my right middle finger in his car door. Before I got inside of my apartment, blood started dripping onto the floor of the elevator and my finger started to swell a bit. How did that happen you might ask? Well....I had to ask him to help me with my bags while getting out of the cab, and he was so busy checking me out and trying to flirt that he wasn't paying attention. He asked if I was okay, and I said, "Well, you knocked off several layers of skin…I can see the white part of my flesh…and blood is starting to ooze out of my finger!" You know this fool had the nerve to say, "Call me. We'll go have Italian food." I thought he was crazy at this point. Did he volunteer to refund the $10.00 cash payment I gave him - $3.00 of which was a tip? No, he did not, and I did not ask. I had his business card from another time he dropped me off – he does unique paintings – on furniture, rugs, etc., and I might know of someone that could use his service in the future – so I kept the card. That fool's card goes in the trash today. Next time I shop at Fig and 7th downtown, I will make sure not to get in his cab.

Oh, it gets better. A few days ago on September, 17, I called to check the balance in my CitiBank checking account and it was short $115.48. This is what happened: I used my Master Card/ debit card on September 16 to pay a bill over the phone. You know how they get the card information then ask for the last three numbers on the back, right? Cool. No problem. But the next day, my account was hit with a purchase from a super warehouse in Florida. I <u>don't</u> shop on line and I don't communicate with anyone in Florida. I reported the fraud to the bank ASAP. CitiBank sent me a new card via FedEx, and I received it the <u>very next day</u>---September 18. The $115.48 was credited back to my account within a couple of business days, and the fraud is being investigated.

I am not rambling. I mentioned these two things to say this: the leaking of this writing, the fraud on my account, and my finger being slammed in a car door [all within a week's time or so] would have probably shut me down about seven years ago. I mean <u>really</u> shut me down to the point where this book would not have been completed. So I am proud to say I have grown in this area.

Sorry about the digression, but I wanted to make a point. Don't let *stuff* shut you down because "*stuff*" is going to happen. Some things are beyond our control at times, and we **must** go on.

I'll share some of what I have accomplished and gained since this writing.

- I have gained ten pounds since June. I weighed 113 pounds when I started writing, I now weigh 123. I have about five pounds to go to get to my desired weight to have my size 6 fit the way I would like. I would have had more weight on, but when I get real upset about *"stuff"* sometimes I lose my appetite. I have been this way since *forever*. I have to work on this too.
- I started working out regularly again. I am not saying I'm ready to start running the steps inside the Metro Rail station on Vermont and Wilshire in Los Angeles yet, but I have started a workout routine. My body is much more toned now---toned enough to where my butt and the back of my thighs can <u>no longer</u> hold the title of *BFF*. That's an accomplishment.
- My hair grew another inch or so. I'll let it grow about three more inches – to the middle of back – that's it.
- My social security payments started in August. I received a back pay of almost $6,000 from them last month, and was able to help my sister, Maja, in Victorville a little bit.
- My landlord had a company put hardwood floors throughout my apartment in July.
- I started going back to church on August 17 (paying tithes, and praying in the Lord's house).

I know you have made accomplishments also. Be proud of yourself. **Keep on your path to excellence**! Stay true to your chosen lifework. This will always take *sincerity*, *truthfulness*, *realness*, and *intelligence*.

Never complain. Always try to find the good in as much as you can. If you don't think you see the good in something that you don't feel quite comfortable with, then try to find the benefit in what occurred. There can be a positive outcome in anything if you want to see it. There is not always a need to intellectualize **each and every** matter or circumstance. The lesson can *sometimes* be noticed immediately. And that is good because something came out of it, right? Better now, than ten years from now! Remember: when you are in a dilemma, be insightful. And if you have to "bounce" something off someone for direction, make sure you have a *trustworthy* source – not someone who will put your business **literally** in the street (not figuratively)! Another point to make: you may have to be "the bigger person" in given situations. You may have to be the better person in moments you never knew. There are some jams in life you **can avoid**. Let petty stuff go!!! In personal relationships, you want to always be as calm as possible in [unpleasant situations]. In business, you want to **always**, **always**, **always** be professional. Even if you feel that certain facts can be predicated on information you have, always be willing [and open] to listen to the other side in discussions.

When I worked as a sales agent in real estate full-time, there was one lender that had four of my deals all at once – all **open** escrows. A lot of money, right? I guess he felt he had me *in a jam*. We were chit-chatting and making small talk one day. He mentioned he had a girlfriend, and he mentioned they went to a church another sister of mine attended. I thought this was nice. Our conversation ended. He went back to his office and called me. He said, "You know I made a pass at you, right?" I said, "No." He then *breaks down* the actual pass he made. I said, "Sorry, I didn't catch it." I thanked him for the compliment, and then said, "Don't you have a girlfriend?" He apparently had a problem after that, and he **stopped** working my deals. I reported this to the owner of the company, but she left it up to him to follow through on his work. Well, he chose not to. Thank god I had good customer service skills, previous banking and lending experience, was excellent when it came to working well with others, and was a professional business person. This man knew I was a single parent, he knew school was about to start, and he knew my son was in private school. And if you're thinking it --- you're right! He was a scandalous person who didn't give a care. *Anyway*, Dorsha Grey got those **deals closed!!! Every single one!!!**

In California, in real estate, this is what I had to do to secure these transactions:

- Prospect
- Get a *strong* lead
- Get the appointment - **Consult/meet** with the buyer (in my office)
- Qualify the client (ensure the client qualified for the loan *first*)
- Research/locate listings
- Call on the availability of the listings (making sure no offers have been accepted)
- Preview the property – if you can (to see if it is within your buyer's interest)
- Show the properties to your client
- Write the offer
- Present the Offer
- Get the offer Accepted
- Open escrow
- Have all disclosures and reports reviewed, signed, and submitted (Transfer Disclosure Statement, Natural Hazard Disclosures, lead-based paint, termite reports, (all required disclosures)…title reports…..
- Have all inspections done within a certain timeframe (usually within the first business week)…Physical Inspection by a **_licensed_** contractor (roof and foundation included), termite inspection, maybe a mold inspection
- Be <u>present</u> for all inspections
- Make sure all parties are *in agreement* to any repairs needed
- Make sure all work is done within the [time specified] and that your client agrees to <u>and</u> is satisfied with the work that was performed
  - Follow through with the **lender** (in this case, what lender?)
  - Follow through with **Escrow** (making sure everything is **on schedule**)

- o Follow through with **Title** (making sure title is **not clouded** and there are **no liens** against the property
- Schedule a final walk-through
- Be present for the final walk-through (so on and so forth).

Hell yeah, Dorsha Grey made sure those transactions closed! All the work you have to do as an agent! And this is just *some* of the work involved in a real estate transaction. This is not all of it! And after all of this, someone at his loan company asked me, "How did you close those deals?" You see, this is why I mentioned early in this book about **patience**, and sometimes you have to exercise even *more patience* when you are looking for a *desired outcome*!

Real estate is a <u>very serious business</u>. While working a transaction, an agent should have a comprehensive **checklist [in the file]** of everything that needs to be done – you cannot "wing it." The transaction file should contain <u>every</u> <u>single</u> <u>document</u> <u>and</u> <u>disclosure</u> needed to close the deal properly, and everything <u>required by the state</u> to protect the client *in place* **[before] the deal is closed**. You have to make sure disclosures are completed <u>properly</u> and make sure all signatures are *in place* **on time**. You pretty much have to oversee the transaction thoroughly and know that **everyone involved** is doing their part when they are <u>supposed</u> to. In short, the ball cannot be dropped, and if it is dropped, you <u>have</u> <u>to</u> <u>know</u> when and why, and make sure the problem is corrected <u>immediately</u>. At my Re/Max office you weren't getting paid on a transaction until everything....<u>every</u> <u>document/disclosure</u> was in place and done <u>correctly</u> – and my files were always complete. I was with Re/Max from 1997 until 2008. I became licensed and active in the business in 1996. Real estate is no joke, and agents and others <u>can be</u> sued. Some states <u>require</u> attorney involvement from the very beginning of the transaction. I have never been sued in this business, and I don't plan to. So as you know, I had to work even harder to make sure the work of the loan officer who was originally involved in these transactions was done properly *and* on time. I had to communicate with other people in his office on these files midway

91

of the escrow and loan process. In addition, I had to put my trust in someone *completely different* when it came to my business and my client. I didn't go whining to my broker – I **had to** handle my business.

You gotta know your stuff in sales. In any business, really, as far as specified knowledge is concerned. Your knowledge should be tight in real estate, you have to stay on your game and stay up to speed with everything – every detail, and you must be prepared and have answers to client's questions when asked, or move your butt and get the correct answer as fast as you can. <u>You must be informed and you must stay current</u>. Whenever a new law comes into effect, or something changes in the industry, you have to be aware of it. It is imperative you know about new laws and changes that could affect buyers and sellers – and sometimes these changes occur mid-transaction. Real estate **is not** a game, and anyone in this industry that doesn't take their job seriously should *consider* getting out of the business. Never work for a broker that doesn't stay current with what is going on in the industry. **<u>Never</u>**.

This happened to me in my second year of real estate. My son was eleven years old. I had only been out of banking for two years. Banking was taking a turn for the worst in the mid 1990's, many banks were merging with others – some were just closing. Our company was part of a merger. After this happened, I decided to take the matter of my future, when it came to earning money for a living, in my own hands, and I wanted as few people as possible involved when it came to a paycheck. I became interested in sales. I acquired a lot of knowledge, and I studied very hard to prepare for the state exam to become a licensed real estate sales person. I was prepared. In 1996, when I took the real estate exam in California, you were given a three hour exam. You had to answer one hundred questions – including mathematical questions. I was very prepared. I took the exam and was done answering the questions within 45 minutes. I carefully reviewed my answers – then I waited until we were dismissed. I passed the exam on the first try! I worked my ass off to learn everything I knew. I listened closely and hung onto every word my broker said. I went to seminars. I listened to motivational speakers. I took even **more** courses. I read many books on the subject of real estate sales from top sales producers. I listened to tapes on perfecting sales skills. I **stayed in** the self-development aisle at Barnes and Noble Booksellers, and I even had a business coach at one point. I wasn't going to just *let* somebody take this away from me. Nobody **gave** me anything. So yes, the deals were closed.

This is why in sales (especially real estate) all of your prospecting material i.e., advertisement used to secure leads, and your communication used in following up with prospects/leads and clients, *should all have [your] direct personal information* (telephone numbers, email address, websites), because *sales is also one of the most cut-throat businesses out there*. And if you're thinking you don't want people to have your cell phone number – then get a cell phone number specifically for work – because others will take your leads/prospects from you if they can and they won't blink an eye while doing it. No lie! I am so serious.

When it comes to <u>my personal life</u>, everything I am mentioning in this book <u>is real</u>, none of it is fiction. None of it. Names have been **omitted** so not to cause problems.

So after coming this far, gaining this much – I let distraction come my way – interfering with my ability to perform at an optimum level as far as getting more sales and reaching my goals. This should not have happened, but it did. It took me a long time to recognize this problem, and after taking a real moment to assess it all, I have to admit that I believe I was seriously depressed – probably to the point where it could have been classified as clinical depression. This was around the period of 2003 until at least 2009. That is a big chunk of time out of my life. Going into what others think and how they treat you. The things they say, and how you interpret what is said, and what it all means in <u>*your mind*</u>. Should I have consulted and worked with a professional conversationalist during this time? I believe I should have. And if I would have been fully aware of what was going on "inside of my head," at an early stage, I would have done so immediately. Regardless, at some point, I should have spoken with a professional, but I didn't know where to turn. I was in the dark. I would have happily given a psychologist/therapist/**life** coach a few hundred dollars for an hour or so a week (or whatever it cost) to help myself. You see, all of the <u>knowledge</u>, <u>seminars</u>, <u>coaches</u>, and <u>motivational speakers</u> do not mean anything, in my opinion, if your head is not right. I feel this way on this subject because **<u>you have to be your best mentally</u>**. It starts with your mind, and if something is stopping you - it needs to be addressed – no matter what it is, and if the problem is this serious in nature, then you have to handle it. Early on, during the years of 2003 to 2005, it would not have been an issue for me to give a professional $12,000 (or whatever) for a few hours a month – to cover a twelve month period to help myself. My money was like that….when I was productive. You think I would not have talked with someone to help myself *and* better myself – to be a [**consistent**] better me? I would not have been ashamed of this. Personally, I would not use anti-depressants for this, but I certainly would have stayed in conversation and close communication with a professional. Don't let yourself ever get in such a fog. Always know how to help yourself mentally and physically, and *<u>stay fit</u>* in these areas. Mentally fit especially!

Think of this: a person can be [told] something that can actually make them faint – their entire body will **collapse**! You can think things that will make your heart "race", sweat starts popping off your forehead, your blood pressure can rise; things can be so **mentally overwhelming** that the body can suffer a heart attack or stroke. And you don't have to be "*old*" in age for this to happen. So yes, how we process information is important. The mind is a very strong force <u>over</u> the body.

Going back to what people say and what people do. A lot of this comes from individuals we are very close to. Many a times, it comes from people we are related to (our actual relatives), and we don't readily understand what is going on in certain situations. I mean, there are a lot of things we don't understand. For instance,

I don't understand how a lot of people under 30 years of age don't like grits. And I also don't understand how a lot of people under age 30 don't know what salmon croquettes are. I grew up on this kind of food and it tastes good to me. I have a box of grits in my house right now. If you haven't tried it, West Angeles Church of God in Christ in Los Angeles serves these dishes for breakfast on Sundays (you can buy breakfast after church service).

Something else I don't understand: why is it that some people seem more <u>content</u> when controversy is present – when negative stimulation is there? I understand that controversy sometimes sells whatever it is a person is trying to promote. And, I do understand that people do what they feel they must to stay present and in the eye of others – but there is healthy controversy, and there is **unhealthy/negative** controversy.

Here is the thing: this book is **not** a religious **[based]** book (religion is not the foundation of this writing). However, I <u>am</u> a Christian, I was raised Christian, and I will <u>always</u> be a Christian. This is not called a *racket* or *fake confidence* - this is my faith. I will **always** believe in God and stay strong and true in this faith, and **absolutely nothing** will take me away from it. <u>**I am not selling Christianity**</u>, and I am not trying to convert anyone into a Christian. Regardless of whether your faith is Catholic, Mormon, or Jehovah's Witness, or even if you don't believe in religion at all, I will still care about you as a human being, and I could still have a friendly conversation with you. People have the faith - or no faith - they **[choose]** to have. Never **[attack]** a person because of their belief system – it is very childish. As long as this person is not hurting you – **don't attack them. We** presently live on **one** planet – **Earth**, and we have to live here **together**. I am not trying to earn money on Christianity here. How you earn your money is your business. Always keep your confidence in your business. Don't let anyone *shake* your confidence or have **you create doubt** in your mind in what **you believe in**. If someone has an opinion and shares an opinion/belief that is not like yours, don't become *alarmed*. Don't have *fear* of this. We were each [created] with a brain – no matter how we became in this **universe**. Don't make me have to love you, because I am not going to hate you. And I am done with this topic!

Family/Relationships. Situations/Problems. Understanding/ Forgiveness.

Today is September 27, and of all I have written to this day, what you are about to read in the rest of this chapter will be the hardest for me to extract from my mind and put to words. As a matter of fact, I cried before I started writing. I am going to make this as concise as possible.

I want to start with this: <u>always</u> remember there are **two sides** to everything when it comes to a relationship.

Learn to <u>listen</u>, <u>understand</u>, <u>forgive</u>, and try not to abandon your family.

The family **unit** is important, and although it can be separate in body – it can still be a unit.

My parents used to have terrible, terrible **loud** arguments, and many, many, days on the way home from school, I would fear something worse happened other than arguing. When I would get to our street, I would walk slower and slower, and when I got to our house, a lot of times, I was afraid to open the door. That's how bad the arguments were. My parents separated when I was twelve years old. My mother took my three younger sisters and <u>just left</u>. Initially, my brothers and I didn't know where our mother and sisters were – they were just gone one day. My mother came to my school and told me what she did and where she and my sisters were. She said she would come back for the rest of us soon. In the meantime, I had to start cooking meals for the family and keep the house clean.

Eventually, my mother ended up coming for us and she took us to a house her new boyfriend rented for her. Her boyfriend never lived in the home with us. All I could think was this: if this relationship ended, what is going to happen to us? After a few years, her boyfriend ended up buying the house we lived in, and by the time I was about 20 years old – their relationship **had ended**. I had to take out a personal loan from Bank of America [where I worked] so we could have money to move because my mother did not have any money saved, and we did not have much notice to move. Anyway, my mother had no idea that the house she rented for us was in a gang infested/drug infested neighborhood – a violent neighborhood. Shit got real. I remember quickly retrieving information from my **[mental]** archive in a serious way. I was second in line. Before we moved, my oldest brother had moved out of the house and with his girlfriend. My father taught my oldest brother and me how to protect ourselves, and how to handle ourselves in many situations. He taught us how to keep a cool and level head in our thinking, how to remain calm in adverse situations, and how <u>not to react</u> in the wrong way. My father used to have weapons. I was taught how to handle and use guns. I knew pressure points and vital areas of the body. I knew how to fight *if I had to*. My father made sure my intellect was sharp. He made sure I had skills. I could actually break someone down *if I had to*. I never knew why he taught me these things at a young age – but he did. My father was fair. His advice was: "Never judge a man, because you have not walked in his shoes. Never kick a man when he is down. Two wrongs don't make a right. There are always two sides to every story, and treat people the way you want to be treated." My father also taught us to *never* hate anyone. He said, "To not like someone is one thing, but never hate anyone." Whenever my father would hear one of his children say they hated someone, he would discipline that child.

At my young age, and with this knowledge, I looked at my new neighborhood and the **situation was not good**. I had five siblings younger than me still in school. I had a full-time job, and I went to college at night. I had to come strong with mine. The first "banger" that parked in front of our door, I told not to park in front of our home **anymore** because there were minor children inside. I took the bus to work because parking in downtown Los Angeles was (and still is) expensive, so I left my car at home, and I asked the guys on the block to watch it for me while I was gone, and not touch it. I was nice and calm in my tone when I spoke with them, and I respected them. I also told them this: "You respect my stuff and I'll respect your stuff. You have weapons, and I have weapons inside." I then said, "Don't let my good looks fool you, and by the way, I have a boyfriend – so don't try to flirt with me, because he wouldn't like it!" They smiled, told me I was a little mean, but they had my back. We were cool from that point forward. But I remember, too many times, hearing guys running alongside of our house at late hours during the night, sounding like they were slaves running for freedom (you could hear them breathing out loud as they ran). Only it wasn't for freedom. These young teenagers and young men were running to escape the police because of the illegal activity they were involved in. I know all *too well* the sound of a police car's engine during a high speed chase. I know what it is like to have helicopters flash lights on your home and in your yard in pursuit of a suspect. I know what it is like to hear gunshots and to hear running feet **stop**. I know what it is like to wake up in the morning – drive around the neighborhood and see chalk lines where a dead body laid, and wonder if it was someone you had seen before. **I know**. I know what it is like to see someone think they don't have **choices** - go the wrong way - looking for a shortcut – only to realize, at the end, there was no shortcut, and their road – their path – ended sooner than they thought. This is when knowledge can hurt and you wish you hadn't known. And you don't have a direct connect to help that person, but maybe someone else did. Maybe someone else had the ability to connect with that individual **but** just **didn't try**. Or, maybe that individual did not want to be connected to [at the time] – feeling they had the answer and wanted to exercise [**the knowledge**] *given* to them as the right choice – only to find - it wasn't.

We lived in that rental house for a little over two years – then moved to a different zip code.

Sometimes you can even move to a different zip code and *stuff* happens. About 16 years ago, my brother Perry and his family lived in a neighborhood that seemed to be pretty decent. Well, I went to visit them one day, and as I was leaving, gun shots started ringing out of nowhere. I was sitting in my car, my brother Perry was standing in his yard, and my sister-in-law and niece were inside of the house. My brother would not get down out of the line of fire. I kept shouting to him to get down, but he wouldn't. The window was shot out of the car parked behind me, but I stayed calm. I wasn't afraid. It was all happening so fast, and all I kept thinking was, if something happened to my brother, what would my mother say – how would she feel? So I got out of the car – ran low in the line of fire – and made my brother get down. Finally, the police came. I asked my brother what was going on. He said, "A drug dealer moved a few doors down." I said to him, "You guys have to move. You can't raise my niece here." Tell me unexpected stuff doesn't happen in life!

All I can say is: look before you leap. Try to get as much information as you can before you make **any** serious move in life. Try to be prepared because you never know when emergencies [that require money] are going to take place. Try to be in a position to help yourself as much as possible, and remember: some things can come to an abrupt ending, so don't just sit there and wait for that train to stop without having a way to continue on your path – especially if you are responsible for others.

I wish my parents could have worked it out, but they didn't. My father began to drink alcohol more, and he became less responsible as far as family matters were concerned. He did not want my mother to work or go to school when they were married. When my parents married, my father was 21 and my mother was 18. My mother had seven children between 1960 and 1969. She did not have the necessary skills to go out on her own to take care of her family financially after she left my father, but she knew she didn't want to be in a verbally abusive relationship anymore. She felt she was protecting herself and the family.

My father wasn't a bad person and he wasn't a bad parent, he just began to lose <u>sight</u> and <u>focus</u> of his priorities in taking care of a family properly. He read us bedtime stories at night. He said prayers with us at night, and he made sure we got good grades in school.

We all know substance abuse can destroy relationships at home <u>and</u> at work. <u>Substance abuse can destroy the home</u>. My father stopped working, and my mother had to get on welfare toward the end of their marriage. So, as I child, I knew what welfare assistance, food stamps, and Medi-Cal was, and I didn't like it. I started working summer jobs when I was 13 years old. We were financially poor, so I qualified for the summer youth work programs offered by the state. When I turned 16 years old, I started working for Burger King (the Crenshaw and Jefferson location in Los Angeles), and when I was in the 12th grade, I started working for AVCO Finance in Inglewood, California (when it was located on Manchester and La Brea). In the 12th grade, I worked for AVCO from 1pm to 5pm Monday through Friday, and I worked for Burger King Friday evenings and weekends. I started working young because I felt that it would be one less child my mother would have to care for financially. So yeah, my life has been a little busy, and it hasn't always been easy.

I said all of that to say this: things happen in relationships and families, but you have to go forward. Forgive, and continue with your loved ones, because everything is not always going to be the way you think it should. And because of how family can be, I have a brother that I haven't seen since 1989. My brother joined the Air Force right after high school. He served the military for four years. I love him, and I really miss him.

In family matters and relationship matters, try not to take sides with people. When I was 24 years old, my father and mother got into a disagreement and I ended up taking her side of the matter because I thought my father was wrong in his actions. I figured I had time to get this straight with him at a later date. My son was only a few months old when this happened. Well, when my son was three years old, I got a call from my grandmother informing me that my father suddenly died (he was only 51 years of age). There was no "later" for me to speak with my father. I never got to say goodbye, and this hurt me so bad. It hurt even more because I failed to remember *there are two sides to everything*. My father never had a chance to meet my son in person.

Try to get the best understanding of problems and situations and learn to forgive as soon as you can. Don't wait for later – because there may not be a later. And that's real.

Relationships have their ups and downs, but if you can work it out – work it out. Seek counseling. Seek all necessary counseling. Drug and alcohol counseling, marriage counseling, counseling for children....seek and get what you need.

People, please don't throw your family away because of situations and problems. **Nothing is perfect**. The people you run to after you leave your family are not perfect, are they? Don't do that. And if you have distance in your family, find a way to contact them as soon as possible (if you are able to) – not later.

Kids (both grown up and minor children) know this: Parents are not perfect. They are people too. Parents fall down too. They may end up drinking too much alcohol, or using the wrong drugs. Adults may end up partying too much after they have children. They may end up with the wrong mate in their life, and may do a little damage to the family because of this. Parents may even end up neglecting the home and spending the *family money* on the wrong things. They can even disappear for a minute trying to escape something, and possibly take the wrong course of action in the process, but this **doesn't** mean they don't love you. **PARENTS [ARE] PEOPLE**. If you are someone that stopped communicating with your parent because of a disagreement you had with them, or because of something they did that *you thought* was wrong – please sit back and [take a real moment] to think. What if *your children (if you have any)* did you the way you are doing your parent now? How would that make you feel? Just think about it, okay?

Don't be afraid of marriage. **All marriages are not bad**. Marriage sometimes take work. A relationship in marriage takes **love, trust, sincerity, [commitment], understanding, care, patience, friendship, and [togetherness] through it all.** And this is just some of it. Marriage is not one-sided. There are two people at the altar when a marriage takes place, correct? You have to be in <u>agreement</u> on a lot of *stuff* in marriage.

My cousin Derrick Grey and his wife, Twanda, have been together since Derrick was 19 years old. Derrick is now 49. Twanda and Derrick have been married since 1992. Their daughter, Tiffany, is 29, their son Donté is 20, and Javon is 19. Tiffany is married, and both of their sons are in college. Donté is studying Computer Science, and Javon is studying to become a social worker. Donté is also into acting. Donté Grey has been in "Orange is the New Black", "Frenemies", "Ghost Stories", and he does commercials.

Derrick and Twanda had their moments, but they are still very much in love and are doing great together. Derrick says, "In marriage you should keep arguments and complaints to a minimum, be very supportive of each other, and communicate." Derrick and Twanda pray together every morning.

Derrick works for AMTRAK, and he is also a licensed contractor in New Haven, Connecticut. He has been remodeling homes for 20 years and he enjoys working on buildings. Twanda and Derrick's home is almost 4,000 square feet, and all of the remodeling to the house they own was done by Derrick himself! Derrick said he is an entrepreneur by heart! So if you need work in the area of contracting, email Derrick at: *brogrey@comcast.net*.

Twanda Grey is self-employed, and her company, Strategic Resolutions, actually ***focuses*** on family life. Strategic Resolutions works with families in need, and the company has contracts with the state of Connecticut to assist in this area. Their slogan is "Building a better you."

Strategic Resolutions specializes in the following areas:

- Support services for children and families
- Parenting
- Clinical Assessments
- Psychotherapy
- Conflict resolutions

Strategic Resolutions' website is *www.strategicresolutionsct.com.*

I would like to dedicate **Eric Benét's song "Real Love"** to Derrick and Twanda Grey.

Ladies and gentlemen let's get a little deep! You want to go forward with as much positivity as possible, right? Well, some things you just have to confront because they are not avoidable. These negative hindering (**sometimes painful**) thoughts will always be in the back of your mind until you *address these issues.* And guess what? Your *[back thoughts]* will eventually become your *[forward thoughts]* - no matter how you try to, or what [you "**use**" to] suppress these thoughts. And with this [**in mind**], there is no way possible for you to be as **effective in a positive [*progressive*] manner** as you would like to be, correct? You may not be able to resolve everything all at once, but work on it! We are all a work in progress, right? This is nothing to be ashamed of. In my opinion, the day you stop being a work in progress is the day you are no longer living. And that, my friend, *is real.*

I pay attention to a lot of things and a lot of people. There are two people that I have had interest in for decades because of their creativity and talent. **They keep it real**, and they appear to be open with their thoughts.

They are Queen Latifah and MC Lyte.

QUEEN LATIFAH is what's happening! I remember when I first heard her. It was the early 1990's, and I was watching a concert special or something on cable television, and all of a sudden, I heard a woman say, "Who you callin' a bitch?" I said, "Whoa, who is that? Let me turn this up!" Well, it was Queen Latifah. She got my attention, and I have been following her ever since. I have not been disappointed in anything I have seen her in, and I enjoy both her rapping and her singing. You can sing Queen! *Go ahead on, girl!!!* You are true to yourself, and on point in your game. Don't stop!!!

MC LYTE. What can I say? Just hearing the name alone you should know. This woman *is* "all that." Her voice is **powerful** – her presence is **strong**! Her rap is **tight**!

MC Lyte has a book titled "Unstoppable: Igniting the Power within to achieve your Greatest Potential." You should check it out.

It would be an honor, an experience, and a great opportunity to hear MC Lyte speak.

LAST ASSIGNMENT: Google MC Lyte. Google Queen Latifah.

The bottom line in Sum it Up is:

- **Know** where you are going.
- Have *and* apply the **correct knowledge**.
- Handle what needs to be addressed to stay **positive** and **go forward.**
- Remain **true** to you!

EIGHT

BE THE BEST YOU

This is the last chapter in this book. Today is September 29, 2014, my father's birthday. Happy birthday Dad! My father would have been 76 years old today.

We would all like to be our best. I haven't met anyone who doesn't. Even if you don't make that thought vocal, deep down inside, you want to be your best. Whatever it is you aspire to do – you want to be excellent. Don't you? Being your best can be a challenge at times, especially when you go through ups and downs, or you get thrown a curve in something you have going on and you go through an emotional/mental setback. Then you find yourself focusing so much on the setback that you can't "get back." We have already gone through this in detail so you know what to do. HANDLE IT!!!

- Continue to wake up positive and <u>focus</u> on being positive.
- Continue to visualize yourself how you would like to be and live.
- Continue to read inspirational literature.
- Listen to motivating and empowering CD's, or watch informative and life/career changing DVD's, or any taped or live media every morning and every evening.

<u>Uplifting reading</u> can be one of your favorite books. <u>Motivating reading</u> can be something *you* wrote down some time ago, and tossed it somewhere because you were having a "bad day." Go find it! Right now!!! I mean it! And if you cannot locate it (for whatever reason), think back and dig deep in your memory - then recreate that writing. Put this beautiful, positive thought that you believe in, in a place where you can see it as often as you need in order to stay inspired.

Personally, I enjoy reading scriptures in the Bible morning and night. I continue to use, to maximum ability, one of the best investments I ever made. That is my subscription to Success magazine. I make sure I listen to the CD's that come with the magazine, and I read the articles of Darren Hardy, John C. Maxwell, and Jason Dorsey regularly. The articles in Success magazine keep me going – **like fuel for my body**. I got my son a subscription to Success magazine over a year ago. He is a young adult in his twenties and he finds the articles and columns in the magazine very helpful and beneficial. I could *hear the smile* in Christopher's voice when I told him I renewed his subscription. The gift of knowledge is an excellent choice to give someone you love.

Continue to read Brian Tracy's book "No Excuses." This is an excellent book on self-discipline and it is easy to read. This book will propel you in a "fast forward" manner to **get stuff done**. I think Brian Tracy's book is *hard core,* and it is not sugar-coated – you *will* move. This book was my personal trainer and coach for a while because it was all I could afford at one point in my life. I love it!

- You want to stay <u>focused</u>.
- You want to have <u>structure</u>.
- You want to have <u>balance</u>.
- You need to be <u>positive</u>.
- You need to <u>stay on track</u> and <u>be committed</u>.
- Stay <u>healthy</u> (mentally and physically).
- If you need a personal trainer for fitness, or a coach for business – get one!

An organization I've used, and will use again is The Landmark Forum. The courses that Landmark offer can really make a difference in your life and your career. I am a licensed real estate sales agent. In the beginning of my sales career, after attending the Landmark Forum, my sales volume increased by 50%. As a new sales agent, I was able to gain the confidence I needed from Landmark. Landmark helps you redefine what is possible and you experience breakthroughs. After participating in Landmark, you will be amazed with the choices you make in every area of your life – not just business. Matters you need closure on, moves you need to make to go forward in relationships, as well as logic and energy you need to advance in projects you're working on. Landmark is there. My broker recommended Landmark to his agents. I am glad I took his advice. Landmark's website is www. landmarkworldwide.com

Make sure you have a level of commitment. Know what you want and where you're going. Have standards. Have a definition as to who you are as a person. Do not let just anyone define who you are. Do not make a practice of settling for less. Use your brain to think, to be, to create. **Be the best you!**

Here are some tips:

- Never become your own opponent.
- Never become your own enemy.
- Never tell yourself what you can't do.
- Never find reasons to not accomplish your goals and be the person you want to be.

I believe the hardest thing about being in a negative/adverse situation is *keeping a positive attitude*. It can be challenging at times. I am not saying it is always easy. Sometimes the simple things can be a little harder because obstacles may be present, and you may have situations that can literally break you down *to your knees* and have you crying like a baby that wants to be pacified. But we have to be strong. We have to persevere. We have to grow and learn from experiences. Experiences are not always mistakes. **Realize. Learn. Grow**. Make steps and strides. Plan to go forward. Arrive in that place of peace and positivity. **Achieve**. And, when you get there….**REJOICE!**

ATTITUDE WITH YOUR ALTITUDE

Rising to the top is great. Success is a wonderful feeling. But remember to be <u>careful</u> on your way up.

Some key things to remember in this area is:

- Do not do anything <u>in the dark</u> that you don't want to see come <u>to the light</u>.
- Do not say anything behind someone's back that you cannot say to their face.
- Treat others the way you would like to be treated.
- Stay out of business that is *not yours*!
- Do not compromise yourself on the way to success! It is not worth it.

It is as simple as that. Because if you don't follow these little rules of life – you may have consequences to pay that you may not be ready to *"pay"* when the bill comes.

I mean, to be in the present, you have to have a past. **Everyone** living in the present has a past – there is no doubt about that. I am saying, *going forward*, try not to have things in your past that you would not like to see.

Presently, if your past is not what you care for, or you have some shame there – don't be ashamed, because you can't change it. **Remember:** we are <u>all</u> a work in progress!

You may have done some things already to get to where you are today – but it *is* [in the past]. You cannot change that. We don't have time machines that would allow us to give our past situations different *"meanings"* for our present. If this time machine exists, I don't know where it is. So we have to deal with it – we have to own it! You cannot run away from it and you cannot let it chase you!

I said that to say this: Don't let **nobody** blackmail you, harm you, or threaten you. Out your own shit if you have to. Don't let nobody profit off your shit! You got people calling newspapers and magazines making money off of you! When they do, you gonna have to talk about it anyway! Hell, you might as well get your story out first *if you can*. They got they tapes of you and whatever else they have?! Well, you know it….and they know it, and they're threatening to let other people know it too, right? Well, you might have to tell that person (or those people) first. [Ask] that person you have to tell to try to [be understanding] – and to be [there] while you are going through this ordeal. What are you going to do? This is where *trust, love, understanding, sincerity of friendship, care, remembering commitment* and staying [*together through it*] comes into play. And if you are in a notable position, (possibly in society, or whatever) you may have to step down. Don't lose your mind, or take your life or someone else's life, or drink yourself to death, or take drugs you don't want to take because you can't cope, or because someone is chasing you. ***Every time you see their number on your phone you cringe. Or, every time you get an email from them – you instantly get a headache or something. Handle it!*** **DO NOT LIVE THIS WAY**. Life is too short already – and you gonna torture yourself? You know you are better than that! You **know** you are. Handle your business in this area so **YOU CAN LIVE**! And if you have to inform the police to protect yourself – do it! A part of law enforcement's job is to serve and protect if someone is threatening to cause you bodily harm.

One more thing:

When you arrive to where you want to be in your success – spend your money wisely and invest properly – so not to have a dim future financially.

- Check out the stock market.

- Real estate **is still** a good investment. Look into it. You have to live somewhere.
- Speak with a financial advisor about what it would take **for you** to have a comfortable retirement **so you won't struggle** with survival in your golden years.
- Don't just give your money away. Give to good causes and charities, but don't throw your money away.

If you have a <u>habit</u> of buying people expensive gifts – *just because*, you might want to think about how often you do this and how much you are spending. I am not trying to limit your thinking, but you never know if something will change in your business or industry and things may start to dry up. What would your savings be like? If you lost everything, and had to end up on someone's sofa because you no longer have your home, how many of those people you are buying lavish gifts for will take you in? And if they take you in, how long could you live with them before you start to get on *their nerves*?

If this is you, are you sitting back asking yourself if you should stop spending so much money unnecessarily because you have doubt in this area? IS FAT GREASY? Hell yeah, you need to slow this down a little bit. I am not trying to tell you how to spend your money, but you might want to a take a [real moment] and re-evaluate some stuff. **Just a thought**.

Remember: I will always care about you. But more importantly, always care about yourself <u>and</u> love who you are.

HAVE AN ABSOLUTELY AMAZING DAY!

I am done with this writing!

Peace and love,

Dorsha

September 30, 2014
dorsha.grey@yahoo.com

ABOUT THE AUTHOR

Dorsha Grey is a business-minded woman who had actively worked in the sales industry for fourteen years. She is a mother, an entrepreneur, and a hardworking woman. She knows what it takes to succeed but, like many, had a few obstacles in her way on her path to success.

After near death, she is ready to get back on track, and she knows what it will take to get there.

Dorsha knows there may be others that are on a quest to success, and she has a few tips to offer. She wants to see you succeed, and she has your back.

Read "I Am Not Finished Yet" on your journey to a better life (a better you).

Made in the USA
Las Vegas, NV
18 March 2022

45874147R00080